THE DENNY LeVETT STORY

as Told by Denny LeVett

THE DENNY LeVETT STORY

as Told by Denny LeVett

Written by

Denny LeVett

CARMEL ◆ PALO ALTO
CALIFORNIA

THE ONLY OFFICIAL, AUTHORIZED BOOK OF DENNY LEVETT'S LIFE STORY

The Denny LeVett Story, as Told by Denny LeVett

Written by Denny LeVett

All Rights Reserved

© 2021 by Denny LeVett

Cover photo by Bill Janes,

Bill Janes Photography, Pacific Grove, CA

All likenesses of Doris Day courtesy of the Doris Day Estate

ISBN 9798722464019

Printed in the United States of America

To my mother,

Eloise Mayburn LeVett

(1911-2003)

and her parents,

Albert Jonathan (A.J.) Strutz

(1890-1971)

and

Retta Marie Strutz

(1891-1985)

— TABLE OF CONTENTS —

— TABLE OF CONTENTS —

— TABLE OF CONTENTS —

ACKNOWLEDGMENTS

The completion of this book would not have been possible without the contributions of many people who are too numerous to mention. To them, I offer my sincerest appreciation and gratitude. However, there are also a few to whom I would like to offer my personal acknowledgment. They include:

Gerard Rose for advising on content and style. Phyllis Mazzocchi for editing, organizing, and making sense of it all. Tony Seton, for encouraging me, back in 2011, to write this book. He recorded and transcribed many of my stories.

And finally, a special thanks to my dear wife Jeanne, my daughters, Amanda and Kate, and all my many friends over the years who have made my life a wonderful experience.

BEGINNINGS

Good Genes

Man, did I get some good genes. My father was D. Frank Kenneth LeVett. Both his parents were French, from the Bordeaux region. I never knew much about them because they both died shortly after I was born.

My father Frank became kind of famous because he was a very good-looking man. In fact, he was *so* good-looking that Chesterfield cigarettes used him as a *Chesterfield Man*. Kinda like the *Marlboro Man*, my father was the *Chesterfield Man*. He would drive his black Chevy panel truck with his picture painted on the side and everybody knew Dad as the *Chesterfield Man*. He'd stop off at all the smoke shops and sell cigarettes. His territory was Iowa, Minnesota, and parts of Wisconsin.

Then one day, sometime after my younger brother Bill was born, my grandfather A.J. asked my father, "Frank, would you come and work in the clothing store? I'll help you buy a house." He said it would be much better for the family if my Dad was around, instead of traveling on the road all the time. I suspect that my father might have had some kind of accident that pushed the point home. And I think my mother had her concerns about him being away so often, too. So my Dad agreed to take the job and spend more time with us.

My Dad was the hail-fellow-well-met sort of man. He was very social, went out to all the parties, had a great personality and told great jokes. The fact was that he partied too much. He died at the age of 49 of cirrhosis of the liver, and that really woke me up. I was just 14 when he died and it was a great loss, not only for me, but also for a lot of people, because he was so popular.

I loved Dad. His time staying at home was wonderful.

He really loved sports, so we did a lot of things together, playing softball or baseball or football every night. Dad didn't hunt and fish, but my maternal grandfather A.J. did.

While my Dad had a boisterous personality, grandfather A.J. was all business. There was no monkeying around with him, other than for hunting and fishing, and basically becoming what was the greatest father figure in the world to me after Dad died.

But great genes came from *both* parents! My Mom, Eloise — what a gal! She was definitely of the *Florodora Girl* flapper style of the 1920s — and what a pistol! She loved to dance and she was just a ball of energy and laughter — a great mom with a great sense of humor. She loved my father, dearly. They were two peas in a pod. When Dad got real sick because he wouldn't stop drinking, it was really tough for her. His death is why I never touched a drink until I was a freshman in college. In high school, when everyone else would drink beer, I never would. While there was always liquor in the house and lots of parties, I'd seen too much partying and raucousness growing up. My grandfather would never speak about my Dad in front of us boys, but he could always be counted on to be there for my Mom, his daughter.

Mom held everything together for us. She loved her two sons. Bill was three years younger than I. He almost didn't make it because he was such a premature baby, and in some ways, he was never really able to catch up. Sadly, Bill died of an apparent heart attack at age 53. He had been working for the government as a teacher at Beale Air Force Base and was eating breakfast and lunch in the cafeteria everyday. Everyone watched as he began to gain weight and get heavier and heavier. I remember the week that he died, there was a big article in the *Chronicle* about men in their 50s, school teachers, dying of heart attacks from the rich cafeteria food. He was a great guy with a great sense of humor. I loved him and always tried to be a good pal to him.

And if you're wondering how I got the nickname

'Denny'—my mother called me *Dennis Albert* when I was bad; *Den*, when she was going about everyday business; and *Denny* when she was happy and proud of me.

Boating with A.J.

My grandfather, I called him A.J. (short for Albert Jonathan, or by 'Strutz,' his last name), was very important to me growing up. Perhaps two stories of how we almost died together—while having fun—might explain some of the closeness in our relationship. Both incidents happened in Canada. Both were in boats.

The first mishap occurred when we were boating on the Kaministiquia River, which is in Ontario, Canada, about twenty miles west of the city of Thunder Bay. We didn't realize that we were so close to the edge of Kakabeka Falls until we saw the foam and spray. Suddenly A.J. said, "Get over to the side, quick! Get over to the shore!" And that's just what we did. Had we hesitated only seconds longer, we'd have gone over the darn waterfall. And that would have been the end of us because it was a hell of a high waterfall. In fact, the Kakabeka Falls drop 130 feet into a gorge. The Falls are called the "Niagara of the North" because they're so beautiful . . . that is, if you don't go over them!

The other unforgettable time was at Thousand Lakes in Upsala, Ontario, when a storm came out of nowhere, causing the waters to get really rough. I was at the motor of our boat. We had only one life jacket. I threw it to my grandfather and said, "Put it on, Strutz. I can swim, you can't." He put in on, just as the engine quit. We were getting swamped; water sloshing over the front and sides—the boat was going down! We had water on the inside right up to the railing. So we're out in the middle of this huge lake, and I remember saying, "Well, Gramp, looks like we're in trouble here. Be seeing you pal." Then I remember seeing the boat kind of go underwater and stop moving. And he was looking at me, and I was looking at him.

"Den, what happened?" he asked.

"A.J., I think we're on a sandbar." We were on a frickin' sandbar! There in the middle of the lake, how do you find a sandbar? But there we were on a sandbar! We were between islands and the sandbar kind of connected one island with the other one. We sat there for quite a while, until a boat came along and rescued our sorry butts! My God! But did we laugh about that later!

My grandfather never drank when he was around me because I was underage and still in high school. But that night he had a shot of whiskey. I will never, ever forget the fear I know we both felt. I can still feel it today.

Bill & Ida Hall

The biggest arms manufacturer, one of the biggest in World War I, was Gaudy Munitions. Gaudy made cannons in Iowa Falls where I grew up. Ida Gaudy was the grown daughter of the cannon maker and she was really quite a gal. I loved her and she was like a second mother to me. Ida never had any children of her own.

She went off to Chicago and became an entertainer and dancer. There she met William (Bill) Turnbull Hall of the *Chicago Tribune* family and they really had quite an affair. He told her he was going to marry her, and he did. Then he was kicked out of the Turnbull family because he married a chorus girl. Bill and Ida moved back to Iowa Falls because Ida had had a great upbringing there.

Bill's brother, Ewert, owned a farm in Iowa Falls. That was kind of an *in thing* at the time; to be a Chicago aristocrat and to own a farm. And if you were going to own a farm, you couldn't do better than to buy one in Iowa Falls, which was truly one of the most beautiful towns in the Midwest. It was called *The Scenic City*. Oh my God! The main bed of the Iowa River came right through Iowa Falls, plus there were other tributaries flowing in. There were 80-foot limestone cliffs and waterfalls everywhere. My grandfather had a home right on one of the main waterfalls at Wildcat Glen.

When 1929 came, old man Gaudy was ruined. Poor Gaudy, he had invested everything into making cannons, but the military was shifting away from cannons to tanks and field guns. He had a couple of big factories in Iowa Falls and he had to close them down. When daughter Ida and her new husband arrived on the scene, I was a little boy I remember Ida would take me over to the east side of Iowa Falls, where the closed-down factories were. Her father lived in a section of one of the factories, but he was very sick and she was taking care of him.

As for Bill, he basically clipped stock coupons. He was still an owner of the *Chicago Tribune* from which he would receive monthly checks, but he no longer had anything to do with the paper. (I recall that Bill had a very wealthy brother, Walter, who ran a newspaper in Massachusetts.)

Bill would go into Chicago on business eight times a year, and once in a while, he would take me with him, even though I was still just a young boy. We would stop off at Marshall Field's—the department store chain since bought by Macy's—and I would get a couple of sets of lead soldiers. Today, I have cabinets full of those soldiers, at home, and at the Cypress Inn, some of which I got more than seven decades ago.

Anyway, the long and the short of it is that Bill and Ida had no children and I was the boy next door. Bill and I would go out to this huge backyard of meadow and forest that stretched all the way to the river that backed up to the end of the property, and we'd shoot rabbits together. Today, you couldn't get me to shoot a rabbit for a thousand bucks! Shooting animals was an awful thing, but I was just a boy back then and living in a different time and a different world.

I shot with a .22, which made it more of a challenge. It was a Winchester Model 97 pump, aught three and aught four, and I was a good shot. Pardon a little bragging, but I used to be able to shoot the head off of a dandelion sitting on my back porch. In those days, you had no problems at all shooting in town. Good old Iowa Falls! It was a way of life. And although I haven't shot animals (just pheasants) since I was a boy, I have not lost my love of guns and have become an avid antique gun collector.

Bill and Ida received all the great magazines, like *Holiday*, which was even published during the last part of World War II. And there was *Collier's* and the *Saturday Evening Post*. I'd go to their house and spend hours paging through the magazines. And every afternoon after school, when I didn't have football, I would read their copy of the *Chicago Tribune*. Okay, I admit it. First I read the funnies. But I was also getting a great cosmopolitan education, seeing all these great places in South America, Europe, and Asia through *Holiday Magazine* and *Collier's*.

My interest in the outside world, enhanced through the magazines, coincided with the end of the war and the return of young men from Europe and the Pacific. There was an economic upturn across the country and it was amazing to watch Iowa Falls absolutely boom!

A funny thing, I'll never forget an advertisement for Hawaii that I saw in one of the magazines right after the war. There was this beautiful, I mean really gorgeous, dark-haired girl, and a headline that read, "Come to Hawaii." I can still see her there in a grass skirt. Oh, how I fell in love with that woman! All my life from then on, I wanted a beautiful, raven-haired beauty as my wife. And what's funny about how some moments can be so important, is that today I am married to that really gorgeous dark-haired woman . . . who then happened to go grey! On purpose!

My wonderful relationship with Bill and Ida lasted until they passed away. I was off on a fishing trip when Bill died and didn't find out until I got back. It was the first loss of someone close to me, since my dad died. Bill was pretty much there all my young life. He was also a good friend of my grandfather Strutz, and a good friend of my father Frank. We always enjoyed Christmas and Thanksgiving together.

Big Sticks in the Water

It was a summer day. It was hot. I dove into the Iowa Falls River and took a swim in the waterfalls. Then I swam over to the boat dock. I noticed several big sticks in the water in front of me. I was almost at the dock, ready to pull myself out, when suddenly, this one "stick" raised its head and turned and looked at me.

Now, we didn't have any water moccasins in the Iowa Falls River that I know of, at least not usually, but I didn't need a close-up to find out. And since I was a pretty good swimmer, I turned around and swam out to the main part of the river so quickly that Johnny Weissmuller couldn't have kept up. Man alive was I scared!

Now, some people might question whether or not it was a water moccasin, but I personally don't know of any other water snake in that area. You usually get water moccasins more to the south, down by the Missouri/Iowa border, in the swamps and so on. Normally, they weren't getting this far north. That particular summer, however, there had been a lot of rain, the water was high, and there had been numerous hot, calm days with no wind to cool things off, at all. Later, I felt vindicated when I heard a radio bulletin warning residents of Iowa Falls to "Watch Out For Water Moccasins!"

A friend of mind, Ben Zigczosky, who was the brother of a girl I was dating, talked about how he often went fishing for walleyes on the North Bend. Once, he hooked what he thought was a walleye, but pulled up a water moccasin, instead. I think he tried to throw it back, but it was still hooked. I recall there were a few other incidences of water moccasins in the area. When the word got around, nobody went swimming in the Iowa River for awhile.

*   *   *   *   *

One spring, when I was in college, I was out with my friends Jerod Trailer, Roger Evans, and Don Seager when I saw a pond that looked like it would be good for fly fishing, something I was good at and enjoyed. Turned out, it wasn't a pond actually, but a bay; some calm water out of the mainstream of the Butte Creek in Northern California. Jerod, Roger, and Don went to the left, I to the right (I don't remember why), but it was a stupid thing for me to do because they knew the territory and I didn't.

Soon, we were out of sight of each other and I continued to walk along the bank, looking for a good place to fish. But the bank rose higher and higher. I kept looking for some place to climb down to the water and fish, but it was a cliff, and at the bottom was the river, which was running pretty fast because of the spring thaw in the Sierra. I was pretty high up and walking close to the edge of the bluff when the ground gave way beneath my feet. I fell, maybe eight feet, and landed on a ledge. Looking around I saw that I was at the mouth of a cave. It was too high to climb back up, and down below were the raging waters of the river.

Then all of a sudden, I heard the *tcheh-tcheh-tcheh* sound that Rainbird watering systems make. But of course, there weren't any Rainbird systems for miles — *that* was the sound of rattlesnakes! I don't know how many, the mind plays games at times, but there were at least four or five that I could see — I didn't stick around to count. I took one deep breath and rolled off the ledge, still holding my rod and reel, and fell about fifteen feet. If I had landed on a rock, it would have been all over. But I landed in the water and seconds later the river carried me over a waterfall, and then another. That's when I lost my rod. I spent the rest of the time trying to keep my head above water and dodge the rocks so I wouldn't bash out the remaining few brains I had left.

Finally, after going over at least three waterfalls and

bypassing lots of rocks in the raging white water down a steep slope, I came into quiet water. There was a beach off to the right. Ironically, this was exactly the sort of pool I had been looking for, just the spot where I wanted to fish. Of course, I didn't have anything to fish with since losing my gear in the rapids, but there was this nice sandy beach with water grasses. I slogged through the shallow water towards the sand, soaking wet and shaking from the cold of the winter run-off, not to mention the experience with the rattlesnakes. (I found out later that the area was famous for rattlesnakes.) Just as I pulled myself on shore, making my way through the reeds, I saw a little water snake swimming in front of me—and I screamed! The snake, I'm sure, wasn't even aware of me, but I can still hear my scream. And I'm not usually a screamer!

My First Gun Show

I started collecting guns when I was nine years old. I was sixteen when I went to my first gun show. It was quite an experience. The gun show was in Deer River, Minnesota, a three-hour drive from Iowa Falls. My maternal grandmother, who was looking after me at the time, was adamant that I shouldn't go. She said it was a waste of time and a waste of money. She told my grandfather not to let me go, but my grandfather said it was okay.

So I left early on a Saturday morning with several suitcases of guns. I was driving an old Chevy for which I had bought some old retreads. I had wanted to get whitewalls to spiff it up, but couldn't find any, so I painted a white stripe around the black wall.

I stayed overnight at a cute, rinky-dink motel that couldn't have cost me more than $10. When I returned home on Sunday night, my grandmother was moaning and groaning. "What are you doing? How come you're home so late? It's a miracle you didn't have an accident." I didn't bother to point out that it was seven o'clock, and it being summer, it was still light out. Instead, I reached into my right pants pocket and pulled out a wad of money that could choke a horse. Then I reached into my left pocket and pulled out another huge wad of money. That quieted my grandmother. My grandfather said, "I'm really proud of you. I knew this was going to happen."

Reflecting upon this experience and the fact that I had never really been to a gun show before, it was just phenomenal. Absolutely phenomenal! It was so exciting to actually have customers buying my guns and paying cash. All right, I had a lot to learn, but this was a good start, and one of the greatest memories of my life.

This was the Mid-West and I was treated very politely. The people there, all of them older than I, were welcoming a new member into the fraternity—the "antique firearm fraternity." This was 1955, and the economy in Iowa, Minnesota, and Wisconsin was booming. People needed hobbies up there. I mean, what else do you do except fight the mosquitoes? They loved gun shows because it gave them a place to go. The fact was that everybody had guns back then because there were no restrictions on who could own what. That's where my machine guns came from. My Sten guns and the Thompsons—they all came from little farm towns because soldiers brought them home from the war. It was easy. As servicemen, nobody was going to search them, or their knapsacks.

I was only a young kid during the Second World War, but I was in my teens during the Korean War; old enough to remember how so many men came home wounded and how families lost their fathers and sons. It was sad. It was really sad.

The Punk Brothers

High school in Iowa was much more my style; more down to earth than Shattuck Military School. And there were important lessons to be learned. My classmate Gary was a *punk*. His younger brother, Jim was one of our high school sports heroes. He was an all-state wrestler, and I didn't want to monkey around with him. Nobody did. But because Jim and Gary were always together, it gave Gary the confidence to think that he could be a tough guy and spout off and bully anyone. I called them the "punk brothers."

It happened that there was a new girl in town. Her name was Marcia, and what a cutie she was. She was adorable. I started to date her a little bit, and we had a good time. We would go to sock hops and rock n' roll dances. We would rock around the clock. Unfortunately, the punk brothers were rockin' around the clock, too. I would be dancing with Marcia when suddenly, the brothers would appear. Gary would try to break in, saying it was his turn to dance with Marcia. And in fact, they got a little rough with me. Gary would taunt me, saying, "Come on, we're gonna step outside to settle this." And I would shoot back, "Hey, I'm not going to mess around with Jim; he's your bodyguard."

It got to the point where things really got pretty edgy. Not being a big guy, I'd developed a theory that I was dead if I didn't show that I was tough. I was with Teddy Roosevelt on this one, that I needed to carry a big stick — well, at least have a loud voice and not let anyone push me around, no matter what. Because if people think they can push you around, they are going to take advantage of you until you've got nothing left.

Of course, if a big guy like Gary beat me up, everybody would think they could fight me. But, if I, *LeVett*, this little twerp of a guy managed to win, they'd find someone else to pick on. So I'd made it a practice in the locker rooms during football season and then basketball that when some bigger guy would swat me with his towel, I'd grab the towel, take it away from him, and give him a shove. That usually ended the swatting, and the bigger they were, the better for me.

Then one day, during football practice, Gary, the "punk," was giving me a real hard time. We had been placed on opposing teams. I was 5'7" and 129 pounds playing defensive back. He was a 5'11" wide receiver. He started tripping me and pushing me around whenever I went for the ball.

Then there suddenly occurred one of those pivotal moments in life! I saw a pass going his way, and I realized, "Denny, if you ever have a chance to intercept a pass, this is it!" This was my lucky day. This was where I was most successful—timing and jumping and catching the ball just before it got to the receiver's hands. And that's just what I did. I caught the ball, brought it down, and immediately Gary tackled me. Then he punched me while I was on the ground. I stood up and he gave me a big shove.

Back then, there were no face guards in helmets, I let him have it. Pow! I buried my fist in his face. It was the best thing I ever did! He just took the punch, but he was so surprised, absolutely shocked that I, in front of everybody, came back and slugged him. Bullies don't like that. But afterwards, the punk brothers never bothered me again. It was an important lesson, for all three of us.

Military School

What would my life story be if I didn't mention having attended military school? I was 15 years old when I attended Shattuck Military Academy in Minnesota. My parents thought it was the right thing to do. Why? Because I stuttered. Yet I was very outgoing. I had my cars, my boats and a great gusto for life. In short, I'm sure I was a handful and my parents thought of me as a pain in the ass. Probably more telling is that my father was in a hospital in Prescott, Arizona, and my mother, who was not only a mother but a school teacher, probably thought I was too much of a wild kid in need of some serious discipline. At least in military school, I would be out of her hair!

I kinda liked military school. For one thing, I was a crack shot, particularly talented shooting a rifle. So they had me on the rifle team. It was interesting that even though I was the smallest man in my squad, I was known as the BAR man. The *BAR*, which stood for Browning Automatic Rifle, was a big, heavy gun (16-24 pounds) that weighed almost as much as *I* did. Everyone else in my unit carried an M-1 Garand (at a measly 9.5 pounds).

Frankly, I was just more fascinated with the BAR than I was with the Garand, and thinking back, maybe I even volunteered to be the BAR man. In war, because the BAR was a serious weapon for defending a squad, the enemy always tried to knock off the BAR man first, so it was an advantage that, by stature, I made for a smaller target. Anyway, this was one place where I excelled.

There was no real social life at military school, at least not for the freshmen, so the place was fun only for a while. I was into sports, of course. At home in Iowa Falls, I was an ice hockey player, so I tried out for the hockey team. I thought I was a pretty good player because I was a pretty good skater and I had grown up playing hockey. But there were other guys who grew up playing the Canucks across the border from Minnesota, and they were like pros. Criminy! I mean, I went out there and was gonna dazzle them with my figure skating and my handling of the puck, but these guys from the border would wind up and shoot a puck a couple of feet off the ice doing 90 miles an hour! I'm thinking, "Oh, oh, I'm way out of my league. This is not for me. I'll be a figure skating champion, not a hockey champion." So my hockey career at Shattuck Military School ended in a matter of minutes. And for those who are reading this and saying, "Tsk, tsk" because I used the word Canucks, "Hey, wake up! That wasn't politically incorrect back then. We didn't even have political incorrectness at that point in time. And by the way, the Vancouver hockey team is called the Canucks. Yep, right out there in the open. So stop your *tsk-ing* and send copies of this book to all your friends to show them how smart you are by telling them about the Vancouver Canucks.

Finally, what I most remember about Shattuck was that I got the mumps and they put me in the infirmary. While bed-ridden, I listened to this radio station out of Minneapolis. Tony Bennett's "Rags to Riches" was the number one hit on the charts and I think I heard it 48 times a day. AM Radio was all we had in those days.

I was only at Shattuck Military School for my Freshman year, and then I came back home to Iowa Falls for the rest of my high school education. How was it, you might ask, that my parents changed their minds and let me go back to the local high school? Because I outright told them I wasn't going to be in military school any longer. That made it simple. And besides, I think they secretly missed me.

The Falls of Iowa Falls

I've spent a lot of my life, as both a boy and an adult, on the waters of Iowa, the Hawkeye State known for its abundance of rivers. Most of that time has been great, but there have been a couple of harrowing moments when things didn't go quite the way I had planned.

I recall it was Independence Day of 1957 when I was the guide of a boat tour through town along the Iowa River for the governor and first lady of Iowa. Iowa Falls is called "The Scenic City," and it is well deserved. The river is bordered on each side by up to eighty-foot limestone cliffs. On one of the cliffs still stands a statue of the great Indian chief, Black Hawk, a warrior of the Sauk Indian tribe, about whom the first Native American autobiography was published in the United States.

So there I was, driving my boat, describing the river, the cliffs, the statue, and the famous cliff pigeons. I shared some of the town's history with the first couple, such as Iowa Falls is one of the oldest towns in Iowa, and that Benjamin I. Talbott, the area's first settler, arrived in 1851. Talbott wanted to name the town Rocksylvania, but was thwarted by later arrivals. The town was plated in 1856 and incorporated as Iowa Falls in May of 1869. I told them about the Indian burial grounds throughout the area. We were in the middle of Indian territory, you know.

So why, you might ask, was I, at eighteen years of age, giving the governor and his wife this tour? Aside from the fact that I was a good speaker when before an audience, having won state and national public speaking competitions, perhaps more important was that I had the best boat in the area. It was a Chris Craft outboard, not inboard, a beautiful boat, with a 50-horsepower Evinrude engine.

What made this particular boat ride significant was that when we were about 25 feet from the dam, with a 20-foot drop to the rocks below, the engine sputtered and died. I knew instantly what the problem was, and without uttering a word, I jumped over the governor and his wife to the back of the boat and switched the fuel tanks. Then I pressed the bulb that would push the fuel toward the engine, and jumped back to the front of the boat. I punched the starter and the engine roared back to life.

We were probably ten feet from going over the dam when I was finally able to turn the boat around, avoiding a catastrophe. I had said excuse me when I hurdled the two of them, and I thought maybe they might have said something to me, if not when it happened, then when the ride was over. Something like, "Denny, good job. You saved us. You saved us from going over the Falls." Or, "Denny, it was brilliant how you did that." But he didn't say a word to me.

I was pretty well proud of myself because the boat and the governor and the first lady and I would've all been goners. I mean, the boat would've been badly smashed up. Those were *big* rocks, and of course the river all around us. So, I quietly said it myself, *to* myself: "Thank you, Denny."

Iowa Falls Aquarama

For many of you, Aquarama might conjure visions of Riva Aquarama's most iconic cruiser. For others, it conjures the commercial passenger ship that toured the Great Lakes after one tour as a troop ship during WWII. For those of us from Iowa Falls, the Aquarama was the biggest event of the summer months.

With all of those rivers in Iowa, we just had to have a good time on the water. In the mid-Fifties, we started an event called Aquarama, which featured a wide display of water sports. It was very popular, and drew crowds from across the state.

I was one of three water ski jumpers, and this was in the early days of water skiing, at least in the mid-West. On one occasion, I lost one of two skis going up the jump. I guess it was too big for my foot. I stumbled slightly, but kept my balance, going over the top on one ski. As I landed, I had the presence of mind to put my free foot on the back of the remaining ski.

It wasn't very pretty. I was all over the place, zig-zagging through the wake of the boat that was towing me, trying to maintain my balance. I must say that I managed to stay up, to considerable applause. Nobody (that I knew, anyway) had ever heard of, let alone witnessed, somebody go over a ski jump on one ski. It was kind of a new thing . . . at least in the mid-West.

Another event in the Aquarama was the pyramid. It would start with three girls skiing. Then two more girls would climb up behind and get on top of them. Then a sixth girl would climb up on *their* backs and form the top of a pyramid. It was very daring and very popular.

I had my own act, which got a lot of attention, especially

on this one occasion. Instead of riding on skis, I rode on a huge saucer. It was a four-foot diameter disk made out of 3/4" plywood that had been varnished and bull-nosed with rounded edges. My trick was to sit on a chair in the middle of the saucer at a small table. I wore a slouch raincoat with a pipe in my mouth and sat there reading a newspaper while I was being tugged along the surface of the water, zigzagging back and forth over the wake and waves.

It was all a matter of keeping my balance, of course, through my feet on the surface of the saucer and through my hips on the seat of the chair. So it was important that my act not start until the water was perfectly calm. However, on this particular 4th of July, Earl Fritz, the emcee, forgot the plan and over the loudspeaker was pressing me to get started. No pun intended, but I was dragging my feet because a speedboat had just gone by towing water skiers, and the surface of the river was too choppy. Earl kept his push for the show to go on; I kept delaying for quieter waters.

It was getting rather embarrassing, so finally I relented and signaled my boat captain to take off. After a few moments of reading my newspaper and drinking my coffee, I started my real act, which was to stand up, put the chair on top of the table, then climb the table to sit on the chair. This, while holding onto the towrope as we splashed along the river.

All was well, until right in front of the grandstands at the marina, the saucer caught the tip of a big wave and I was thrown up into the air and then cast downward into the water. I hadn't realized how shallow this water was until I found myself head first and shoulder deep in the mud, with my butt in the air.

I will never forget pulling myself out of that mud and righting myself in the water. Some kid was yelling, "His face is all mud!" I'll never know how I had the presence of mind to wipe that mud out of my eyes, stretch out my arms and go straight into a rendition of "My Mammy . . . I'd walk a million miles, for one of your smiles. My Maaaammy!" (I do a mean Al Jolson.)

The audience went crazy, and Earl Fritz said something like, "Of course, it was all rehearsed this way." All's well that ends well in show business!

From Stutterer to Speechifier

I've been speaking before audiences for more than half-a-century. It's one of my favorite things to do. Even more than public speaking, though, being an entertainer has been in my blood since before I can remember. But my acting career took a hiatus when I developed a serious stutter during my grade school years. I got it because of my maternal grandmother, Marie. She had the habit of always stopping me in the middle of what I was saying and making me start over. That's when I started shuttering. The interesting thing was, I was fine speaking in front of the rest of my family. It was just my grandmother. Her mere presence made me nervous . . . until it wasn't just my grandmother anymore. She had succeeded in eroding my self-confidence until I also began to stutter when I was in a situation like speaking in front of the class. I would get nervous and stutter.

It wasn't until my high school years, when I was acting on stage, that I discovered my stutter went away when I went into character. My 'characters' did not stutter. In fact, when I acted, I could become a veritable Demosthenes, a Winston Churchill, or a Martin Luther King. Characters in plays did not stutter.

This breakthrough occurred because my high school speech and drama teacher, John Connor, took the time and interest to guide me through this awful period of my life. He saw the possibilities in me, and gave me the self-confidence I needed to push through.

He gave me all the best parts in the school plays, and by my senior year, I was starring in productions like "Gertrude the Governess" and "Cyrano de Bergerac." I also became the class emcee. Even after Mr. Connor moved on to Ellsworth College, he still cast me in all the plays there. He also made me the college emcee and rally commissioner.

When I began college at the University of Iowa, I met Dr. Wendell Johnson, a world-renowned expert in speech therapy. He took a real liking to me. He was intrigued by the fact that when acting, I didn't stutter and that as a young child, I had never stuttered. He was the one who helped me identify when, why, and how it all started. Dr. Johnson had me speak in front of a mirror, and count the times I had vocalized pauses; saying things like "ah" or "um" or "er." Then after I counted the vocalized pauses, he said, "Why does that bother you, Denny? Everybody does that. You shouldn't feel self-conscious."

I would deliver speeches in front of him, and he would say, "There wasn't one vocalized pause, Denny, not one." He had given me the confidence that my grandmother had taken away; all the confidence in the world to realize that I didn't have to stutter. And then he said, "You know. Denny, you are not a stutterer."

All of a sudden, one morning I got up and said to myself, "All right, I don't think I stutter anymore." And you know what? I didn't. I then went on to enter public speaking contests and won quite a number of them.

I remember one in particular. It was the state-level competition of the National Iowa After Dinner Speaking Championship. I wrote my own script, of course. It was a take-off on Dale Carnegie's "How to Win Friends and Influence People." I titled it "How to Lose Friends and Alienate People," and declared it "dedicated to a man who didn't really need it, Adolph Hitler." It was funny, and I won the competition. I was 18. It was prologue to a number of public speaking awards to come.

In fact, my acting and public speaking work really paid off for me. Not only were there plays, including a number of musicals, but I also appeared in some television commercials. The television business was just beginning to take off. My family had just bought our first TV set, and now, my first professional gig was acting in a television commercial. These commercials were some of the first ever travel ads made for broadcast. I recall that one of my lines was the most important hook in the commercial, "Going? Go Greyhound."

For my sophomore year, I transferred to the University of the Pacific (UOP), in Stockton, California. There, not only was I one of the top leads in every play, but I became the local rally commissioner, a frequent speaker at college events, and a stand-up comic. Yes, comedy was my thing. I loved getting laughs from an audience—any audience. In all my speeches, particularly in politics, I would use humor to engage the crowd; to get them on my side so they could take the serious stuff and see it in a more favorable light. I do that to this day.

Mostly when I prepare to deliver a speech, I don't write it out. I make notes and then try not to use them. I figure that a sign of a good speaker is no notes. That way I can listen more and play off the audience. But one of my favorite little tricks is that when I do use my notes, or refer to them too often, I apologize for even having notes. Then I will peer down at them, and as though I am reading the notes, I'll say, "Seafood." Next, I'll pause and look confused. Then, as if a light just went on, I'll say, "I'm sorry. That's not seafood—it says *see footnote.*" That usually brings the house down.

* * * * *

A postscript. Public speaking can really take you places. It was in my first year at the University of Iowa that I met the future actress Jean Seberg, who had also won a speech contest. She approached me after one of my speeches to introduce herself. She was a gorgeous gal and we started dating. She lived in Marshalltown, Iowa, which is about 50 miles from where I lived at a time when we didn't have the highways that we do today. It was a long ride.

The relationship was going well, or so I thought, when she invited me to her parents' home for Thanksgiving. When

I arrived, she introduced me to François Moreuil, her French boyfriend, whom she would marry a year or so later. I decided I didn't need to stay, so I made some excuse and headed back to Iowa Falls, getting there just in time to have Thanksgiving dinner with my own parents.

Reading up on Jean Seberg, I was reminded that she had been chosen by Otto Preminger to play the starring role in his film, "Saint Jean," about Jean d'Arc. Jean had been selected after a high-priced, high-visibility, nationwide talent search. She hadn't acted before, except in school. Both the film and her performance received poor reviews. She later said she had two memories of the film. One was being burned at the stake in the movie. The second was being burned at the stake by the critics.

A Year Abroad

In mid-August of 1959, students from University of the Pacific, Chico State, University of Alabama, and University of Georgia boarded the *USS Atlantic* departing from New York harbor. We had two weeks of onboard classes on our way to Western Europe via Belgium where we drank in the sea air at Zeebrugge before making our way to Amsterdam, the most liberal city in the world and our home base for September and October of that year.

The Hotel Isabella on Spiegelstraadt was sensational. We took over the entire establishment for two months and set up classrooms in-house. While there, we took the opportunity to soak in the culture; attending the Opera, sightseeing the fabulous architecture, learning about the local horticulture, and visiting some of the greatest art venues in the world, including the Rembrandt and Van Gogh Museums. And of course, we couldn't overlook Amsterdam's equally famous Red Light District, but that's for another book.

From Amsterdam, six of us took a short trip to Düsseldorf, Germany, and back. At the Volkswagen factory there, where we bought six Volkswagen buses that we drove back to Amsterdam to pick up our fellow students and drive through Germany and Switzerland to Austria. Austria would be our base for November and December. In Vienna, we stayed at a hotel in Bad Voeslau, near an old Luftwaffe Air Base. The base's claim to fame in those days was *grouse*, a game bird that we hunted every day.

Each and every night, we attended an opera in Vienna — and let me tell you, those operas were magnificent! Indeed, looking back, these experiences in Austria made for some of the greatest times of my life.

On returning to Amsterdam, I spent most of my time

purchasing classic cars and antique guns, including a 1933 MGJ3, a 1936 MGTA, and a 1948 MGTC.

I recall that Professor Oliver from Chico State, who was running the classes, got pissed off at several of us for not being more diligent with our studies and for partying too much. He said to three of us, "You're a bad representation of American students." Plus, he complained that our carousing was a bad influence on the rest of the students, not to mention the attention I paid to making money and buying things. We were more trouble than we were worth, he said, at the ripe old age of twenty. We were asked to jump ship, so to speak.

When I came through customs in New York City, I had two suitcases full of antique guns (pre-1898) and no clothes. I had sold all my clothes or given them away. Thankfully, I got a customs guy who was really into antique guns. He looked at them, spent a little time with me, and wished me the best. I told him what I had paid for some of them—$5 here, $25 there—and he said he was inspired to go to Europe and buy some guns himself. This was in 1959-60, not long after WWII and the Korean War, so there were guns everywhere.

*　　*　　*　　*　　*

Oh, the things that I learned in Europe! Amsterdam is where I bought my three MG's. I made a lot of friends there, including Vim Bosma, the owner of the Airliner Nightclub, which catered to stewardesses and pilots—a hot, hot place. Vim also had several antique stores and lots of antique guns.

Ironically, what you couldn't put your hands on, even in Amsterdam, was a modern gun. You couldn't even get a permit for one at that time. But everybody who couldn't get one wanted one—and that included Vim; he wanted lots of them. Now, not that I knew Vim was using stewardesses and pilots to smuggle, but I had my suspicions. That's when I thought, who better than a student! So, I began smuggling modern guns from Italy, where anyone could buy anything, to Amsterdam, where I traded with Vim for some of his antique guns. This was a great boon to my early collecting.

I had a strategy, too. I figured that because Bernardelli handguns were made in Genoa, and Berettas made in Milano, that I would take the train to those places and buy guns. I would go into a local bar and place a sign on the table that read "Will Pay $5 for any Bernardelli or Beretta." All kinds of people brought me guns. All I had to do was peel off a $5 bill and I would have a gun.

I always put the guns in my riding boots, which back then we carried over our shoulders on straps. Then I would stuff my underwear on top of the guns and take the train back up to Amsterdam. I would either sell them to Vim for $50 a piece, or trade for his antique guns. At that point, I even thought of making my career out of buying and selling guns.

I had a pretty good business going until one day as I passed through a train station in Germany, where the Customs Inspector recognized me. He searched me, but thankfully, did not search my boots. The inspector wanted to detain me right then and there, but the Conductor argued that I could not get off the train simply because the Germans *thought* I was smuggling something, without any evidence to back it up. I was ordered to remain confined in my train compartment until I reached my destination, which was Amsterdam. Phew!

*   *   *   *   *

At the time, Holland, which is still known as a major diamond-trading center, was the heart of the global diamond cutting industry. I decided that I wanted to learn about, and buy, diamonds, so, I went directly to the cutters in Antwerp to do my business. In those days, at least, they'd save some of the cutting leftovers for themselves and shape them into smaller stones. The ones that I bought weren't big, but they were so expertly cut that they were still larger than a half-carat. As a result, I now had my own stash of diamonds that I had bought for only around $50 a piece.

When in Madrid, I continued my quest to buy antique guns. One day, as I was walking towards an antique shop there, a scrubby looking fellow walked up to me, and said in broken English, "Diamond?"

Taken aback at his question, I replied, "Real diamond? Where did it come from?"

"A lady," he said.

"Oh, really. How did you get it?"

"It came from lady. Real diamond," he insisted.

I took it in my hand and tried to get a good look at it, and then, I purposely dropped it. I knew that if it wasn't a real diamond, it would break.

The man screamed, "Oh, no!" as it broke.

I thought the poor guy was going to cry. I said to him, "This is no diamond. This is glass. Glass!" I thought it was so clever of me. Oh, I thought I was cool at 20 years old. Fortunately, there were people around, so he didn't try to kill me.

At that point in my life, I would do anything for adventure. I had seen movies of heroes who smuggled, but I was never worried about being arrested. I didn't even think about it. I was a college kid. I figured that if I got in trouble, I could always go to the American Embassy and be safe. And no, just in case you're wondering, I don't think I'd find myself doing the same things now, as I did when I was 20. Back then, I think I had a sense that I would never be able to repeat the experience I was enjoying on the Continent. Here was Europe in 1959, still recovering from World War II and re-building economies. Everything was ten cents on the dollar. Prices there were so reasonable that you could have a wonderful dinner in Vienna for just $5. In fact, that might have even been considered a little expensive.

At that wonderful hotel in Bad Voslau, they would cook up the grouse I had shot the same day. We would eat dinner, and then spend hours drinking at the bar every night and smoking cigarettes, which in those days is what college kids did. The French Gitaines were a favorite.

Americans were very popular in Europe at this time. Maybe not quite so popular in Germany, of course, as I found out traveling through that country, but certainly in Holland, France, Belgium, and Italy. We were Kings! But while we were so admired, and looked like such clean-cut guys, we managed to mess all that up, because we became arrogant. We were so patriotic and so nationalistic, that as Americans, we thought we were absolutely superhuman.

Frankly, I don't think the way we treated other people was very nice at all. I think we were brash and rude, on top of the arrogance. Unfortunately, I didn't see it at the time because I was there, and I was a part of it. But the pride, the nationalism, was a powerful feeling. Oh, how we loved being Americans in Europe!

The first thing I would say when I met someone was, "Hi, I'm Denny LeVett. I'm an American." We were like an invincible race.

They were awfully nice to us in Austria, I'll say that. We went to school there, lived with the locals and got to know so much about them. Oh, it was a terrific way to learn, but unfortunately, I think we ruined it in the long run by giving people there the impression that we were greedy, egotistic Americans.

When I next spoke to my grandfather, A.J., and filled him in on how I was able to buy cars, diamonds, and two suitcases of antique guns, he told me it was always better to travel by train in Europe than by car. The railway system was, and still is, extensive, going just about anywhere you want to go, and making travel so easy.

Sure, driving the roadways was wonderful, but nothing was more beautiful than the Rheingold Express, which left Amsterdam at 8 o'clock in the morning and arrived in Lake Como, Italy, at 9:20 in the evening. If you drove that same route by car, it would take you a full two and a half days to get all the way to Como from Amsterdam. The Rheingold Express had observation compartments with glass roofs that gave spectacular views and ran right up along the edge of the Rhine River. Just stunning!

Back to School

It was cool then, going back to COP (College of the Pacific) after my trip to Europe. I was older and wiser, with much more to talk about, making for interesting listening, especially among the COP women who hadn't been there. They were fascinated with me because I had spent school time traveling there, and I definitely played it up—all those wonderful times in Amsterdam, Vienna, and Florence.

I only made the honor roll twice in my life. The first time was during my senior year in high school. So I was determined that I was going to make the honor roll for a second time in my senior year in college. I was successful, probably in part, because I was taking courses that I absolutely loved. Making the honor roll at COP turned out to be a big deal in my life. My grandfather and mother were so pleased. They recognized a major difference between the 18-year-old boy who left for college and the 21-year-old man rising to the fore. I was a different person, and if I do say so myself, I had become a pretty darn popular man around campus. In addition to my arsenal of European stories and the status of making honor roll, I was the college comedian, actor, dancer, and cheerleader. That meant I always had cute girlfriends. Yes, I guess you could say I was a big man on campus. And at this point, I knew for certain that I wanted three things in my life—fame, sex and money!

After that European trip, I became very serious about a career in business. I had one more year to go at COP because out of the 33 units I was supposed to earn abroad, I had only been given three. But my experience in Europe—the opera, the music, the galleries, the artwork—was probably the greatest education I could ever have had—worth 2,000 credits at least! It was the best thing that ever happened in my young life. My grandfather, A.J., had helped me pay for college, and I had a pretty good stash of money saved up from selling guns. I owned some stock that he had recommended, plus I'd sold my 1957 Chevy convertible and made a big sale on that. What additional money I didn't have when I needed it, my grandfather picked up for me. He would loan me the money.

I had a little gun business on campus. Back then it was legal. No problem at all selling a gun to anybody who wanted one. Guns were regarded differently back then. More like a hobby. There was no stigma to owning one. But then, people weren't going on campus shooting with automatic weapons, like now. It was a different world. At least that's how it seems, looking back.

In order to make ends meet, I also worked during my senior year; hashing and serving food and washing dishes at the fraternity house. That was a good experience because it taught me that I never wanted to own a restaurant and never wanted to be a server. *(So where am I sitting right now? In my restaurant at the Cypress Inn. An important lesson to unlearn!)*

Looking Good

My attire has always been important to me; it's been a lifelong issue. My Grandfather, A.J., was the most dapper man you have ever seen. Always dressed to perfection. From the bow ties, to the silk handkerchief in the pocket, to the Alpagora suits. Of course, it helped that he owned a very large clothing store.

A.J. was quite an entrepreneur. He built his own building, which not only had a clothing store on the street front, but apartments up above. The first floor of the store was all work clothes. My Grandfather had the first retail shop in the state to carry Levi's. He also had the popular bib overalls; Oshkosh and Wrangler brands, et cetera. The second floor of the store was all formal suits and ties and dress shirts. In the mezzanine were sport shirts, shorts and children's wear. So it was a complete one-stop shop for men and children, with a few Levi's jeans for women.

At that time, Iowa Falls was the central hub for approximately 60 farm towns. It was by far the biggest township around, but wasn't populated by much more than maybe 7,500 people. However, it was very prosperous for such a small town, and the only place in Northern Iowa where you could find children's clothes. Otherwise, people had to go to Des Moines, Marshalltown, and Waterloo to garb their children.

My grandfather had a very successful clothing business, so naturally, he taught me how to dress. And when pink was really popular, around 1955-56, I had the most beautiful, worsted wool pink sport coat. Think *Sha Na Na*. I was the first kid to have a white sport coat and a white dinner jacket during my senior year in high school. I still have the white jacket, if you can believe it — and it still fits beautifully.

My grandfather, A.J., had a lasting effect, because to this day, it is still important for me to look good. Maybe it's just me showing myself off in an artistic way, or showing respect for where I'm going, or who I'm seeing. I think it's a matter of habit. I've always tried to look good. If anyone is going to overdress for an occasion, it will be me—whether it be a formal dinner, or a fishing trip.

My grandfather liked to say that clothes make the man, a saying I wouldn't really understand until I got older. It was then that I began noticing what other people were wearing. If someone tried to look sophisticated, I noted that it added credentials to their business image. In this way, I think my grandfather wanted to be dressed so that people would listen to him and pay attention. And I have to say that I have more respect for someone who wants to be a leader and takes the time and attention to dress well. Indeed, I personally believe that you can never be overdressed.

An example of this is the case of Dan Lungren, the former California Secretary of State, who ran against Gray Davis for governor in 1998. I was president of the Northern California Lincoln Club, which meant that I was involved with the Republican candidates. This was a time when I was trying to get the Lincoln Club and the California Republican Party to go middle of the road. Here in the Golden State, you had to take a moderate position if you wanted to have a chance at being elected. If you were not moderate, your campaign would go down the toilet.

Lungren was very, very pro-life, to the point where he would lecture women about it. There were several pro-choice candidates running, as well. So, I would say to Dan, "For God's sake! Knock off the lecture. Right now you've got a reprieve because people are saying it's your religion; it's because you're Catholic. But don't push it. Don't lecture." Unfortunately, Dan couldn't help himself. He was just that kinda guy.

But that's not why I'm telling this story. I'm telling this story because Lungren was the worst dresser you ever saw in your entire life! People running for public office should dress impeccably, or at least make a serious effort at looking good. Maybe it shouldn't matter, but it does. People notice appearance, even if they are not conscious of it. Lungren didn't even make an effort, at least that's how he appeared. He would have socks that drooped down with balls on 'em. Shoes that were kinda like the old army shoes that needed polishing. Sport coats that were shiny material. Ties that didn't even come close to matching his shirt and coat. This was somebody who didn't spend any money on clothes, and he really needed to. He was a public figure; a guy you'd expect to pay attention to his appearance.

Tom Campbell was another public figure who didn't dress well. Not as bad as Lungren, but he didn't know how to make himself look good. I'd talk to him all the time. I told him, "Wear blue blazers. Don't go grey." Tom always wore grey suits. Men should never wear grey. I love silver and grey, but not on a man. I think I might have made a bit of a mark, because I finally got him to start wearing blue blazers.

I know it shouldn't make that much of a difference when someone doesn't pay attention to appearance, whether a businessperson or politician, but it does. It can show their self-awareness. It can say that they don't care what they look like. Or, that they don't know better. And for a politician, it might raise questions about what else he or she doesn't know.

Dance Halls and Lakes

Growing up, we had a wonderful lake that I always went to, which was Clear Lake, Iowa. Our house was right above Wild Cat Cave. We called it Wild Cat Glen. My grandfather's house was right nearby. It was beautiful. About two and a half hours northwest of Clear Lake is Lake Okoboji, which is one of three blue water lakes in the world. The other two are Lake Louise in Banff and Lake Lucerne in Switzerland. It's a scientific thing. They regurgitate three to four times a year. The springs and artesian wells turn over the water, which makes it so pure and so clear.

There were dance halls on the shores of Lake Okoboji, Clear Lake, and even my hometown of Iowa Falls where only a fifteen minute drive away was Siloam Springs with a grand ballroom where the big bands performed. Of course, back during the 30s, 40s and 50s, that was our live music. Every Monday night there was a 30-piece orchestra. Band directors from all over Iowa came to Okoboji on Monday nights to play at the inn.

Clear Lake was shallow and filled with a lot of weeds. It wasn't a great place to swim, but it did have the Surf Ballroom—a fun place to go to that attracted great talent. I grew up 40 miles away, so it would take me 45 minutes to an hour to get there. It's where we all hung out as kids. The Surf Ballroom is where Buddy Holly, the Big Bopper, and Richie Valens played on that fatal night. Tragically, when they left early the next morning, their plane crashed and they were all killed, along with the pilot.

My friend Nancy Krause, who I grew up next to in Iowa Falls, moved her summer home from Clear Lake to Okoboji. She planned a reunion there for the weekend of July 10th of 1986. At the time, I couldn't make it because my then-wife

Karen, a former schoolteacher and interior decorator, was very pregnant with my youngest daughter, Kate. In fact, Kate was born that very day. I remember it well because child-bearing age in Iowa back then was between 16 and 19, and everyone was asking me if it was my daughter who was having a child. (Cough, cough). Anyway, in August, that same year when Kate was a screaming infant, Nancy had another reunion that was mostly for the group of people who'd gone to kindergarten together, some 45 years earlier. Those people were among my best friends, so I had to go back to Okoboji for it. I decided to take my mother and my brother along with me. It was my first trip back there since I was in high school. It was like going back in time.

When we drove into Okoboji, the first car I saw was a red 1948 MG TC driving along Lakeshore Drive. A few cars later was a 1955 Ford Crown Victoria station wagon. And then, shortly after that was a red and white 1955 Chevrolet Bel Air convertible. It was amazing. We got to Nancy's house — she still has that house — and went down to the lake for cocktails where there were old Chris-Crafts and Century Boats all over the water. I couldn't believe it! I've got the only Garwood in Okoboji. I was lovin' it right away.

When we went out to Maxwell's, which was on the top floor at the Emporium, it was just about sunset and I was looking out at this unbelievable scene of boats everywhere. Okoboji that evening was the most beautiful place I've ever seen in my life. It was just heaven.

In Okoboji, there is also an amusement park with one of the oldest roller coasters in America. There is a Roof Garden where Doris Day once sang — and where just a couple of nights later, I danced to Bobby Vee and the Crickets. In those days, Okoboji was something else!

*   *   *   *   *

Just a postscript . . . that first kindergarten reunion was over thirty years ago when I was at an age where I could really appreciate it. Knowing back then that there would be many more kindergarten reunions to come, when I went back that Fall, I bought a house on the lake for just $35,000. That's all it took!

THE BUSINESSMAN

Rags to Riches

In my senior year, University of Pacific began offering real estate classes for the very first time. The classes were taught by a Professor Brumbaugh, a Stockton real estate broker who changed my life—and I thank my lucky stars for that professor! Brumbaugh's "Theory of How to Become a Millionaire?" Buy a duplex, triplex, fourplex, or five unit complex, and live in one unit while renting out the others. And always use someone else's money! A bank loan required 10 to 20 percent down, based upon a residential property. With an 80% loan from the bank, using the rental income from the building as proof of cash flow, borrow the 10% from family or friends, then get a partner to come in on the deal for the remaining 10%, and you are 100% covered. Moral of the story? Someone else's money is buying that property for you.

Professor Brumbaugh must have sensed some potential in me, because he made me a deal—if I would get my real estate license, he would give me an 'A'. When I asked him what town he would recommend to buy in, he suggested a college town, like Palo Alto. The seed was planted. After a stint at Stanford Business School, my girlfriend Ruth suggested I take a job in her father's real estate office while I waited to enter the Northwest Orient aviation program, which at the time, was my dream job. My first deal came straightaway, with a profit of $600. This was equivalent to two months' salary at Northwest Airlines back then. I didn't realize there was so much money to be made in real estate and I quickly determined that real estate was the way for me to go. I hastily sent a resignation letter to Northwest before I ever piloted a flight. Then with that $600 commission, I put Professor Brumbaugh's training into action and in February

1961, I bought my first duplex in Palo Alto. I lived in one unit and rented the other. I was 21 years old and you can't imagine how that changed my life. I got responsible pretty quick. Two months later, I bought a four-plex, moved into one of the units and rented out the rest. I did all the painting, plumbing and remodeling myself. It was just so gratifying to stand back and say "now I own *two*." Being in an area like Palo Alto, when it was just taking off, was the luckiest thing that ever happened to me. It wasn't long before I became a full partner in the California Lands Investment Company, and from thereon, I was on my way!

My grandfather, A.J., was extremely influential in my life. Being from the Midwest, he had modest values. He told me never to act like I had more than $25 in my pocket. He was from the banking business and taught me the importance of working with banks and to establish good banking relationships. I followed his advice, and secured a short-term, 90-day loan at the very beginning. I didn't need it, but it established my credit with Bank of America. People tell me I own residential downtown Palo Alto, but I don't like to be referred to this way. I just see that so many people in Palo Alto like the intimacy of a small, charming building, and I work to give them that.

Ruth and I had a brief marriage during this time period, when a little bit soused and on a dare from our friends, we drove to Reno one night and got married. We were young and impulsive and it was over in six months, but we remained great friends afterwards.

In 1972, I purchased the Benbow Inn in Garberville, California, a small town in the heart of Redwood country near the Eel River in Humboldt County. How did I get from Palo Alto to Garberville? Well, I was already somewhat familiar with this area from my teens, taking road trips with my grandfather A.J., who had left Iowa Falls to join the family in Gridley, California, where my mom taught school in nearby Yuba City. Grand-dad liked to take my brother Bill and me salmon fishing at Coos Bay, Oregon, off Highway

101. We'd jump in the car and drive all the way north through California into Oregon. I recall once catching a 38 pound salmon in the bay. It took me half an hour to reel it in, and then I ended up feeling sorry for the fish. As fortune would have it, many years later, in 1972, while driving along Highway 101 in Humboldt County and looking for a place to stay overnight, I made a stop at the Benbow Inn in Garberville. Well, I fell in love with it, immediately! The inn was built in 1926 of Douglas Fir in the Tudor Revival style and is beautifully situated on the Redwood Highway with convenient access to the Avenue of the Giants. At the time, the inn was owned by Art and Claudia Stadler, and we ended up making a deal. The Stadlers would later become like a second family to me, as what began as a business transaction, led to a long and dear relationship.

I have indelible memories of listening to Harry Owens and the Royal Hawaiian Band singing "My Isle of Golden Dreams" on the juke box at the Benbow Inn, and of the popular golf tournaments we held there every year. I even won a tournament once! The inn was renowned for its celebrity clientele, including Spencer Tracy, Clark Gable, and even Eleanor Roosevelt. It was subsequently listed on the National Register of Historic Places in 1983. I owned and operated the Benbow Inn from 1972 to 1978.

I later expanded my real estate holdings to residential units and inns in the charming Carmel-by-the-Sea, poised on the west coast of the Monterey Peninsula.

So how did I get from Garberville and Palo Alto to Carmel? Well, my friend Chuck Watts, who owned the Vagabond House Inn on Dolores Street in Carmel-by-the-Sea had his eyes set on buying the Benbow Inn from me for quite awhile. He was always trying to get me to visit Carmel to talk it over. As it turned out, there came the day when my then girlfriend Barbara, was practicing to get her diver's license over at Monastery Beach in Carmel. I called Chuck for a place to stay and he put us in a room at the Vagabond House Inn. I recall it was a Saturday, December 10th, for two nights. Well, I loved the Vagabond House Inn right away. Chuck and I negotiated a trade deal where he bought the Benbow Inn and I bought the Vagabond with a 3 million dollar note and deeded trust. Today, the Vagabond House Inn is one of the most popular inns in Carmel. (But more on the Vagabond House, later.)

I went on to purchase dozens of residential units and a number of boutique hotels and inns in Carmel-by-the Sea, including the Cypress Inn, the Lamplighter Inn, Monte Verde Inn, Casa De Carmel, Vagabond's House Inn, and the Forest Lodge.

In collaboration with a talented partner, Chris Tescher, I am also a builder of houses. Sometimes, we purchase a property and tear it down to rebuild, and sometimes, we start from scratch. My favorite of all the houses we have built is located on 17 Mile Drive in Pebble Beach and is a replica of a Cape Dutch Style house that I first spotted on a trip to South Africa.

My words of advice for those just starting out? First and foremost, buy in the best possible location. My niche is 4-to-12 unit properties within walking distance to downtown restaurants. Second, stay with what you know. I've always liked small, charming properties. Third, research and do your due diligence. And fourth, work with a good financial institution. Rule for myself: I don't sell one property unless I can buy *two* more with the money!

As long as you've got good credit or the ability to get money, do what you can—beg, borrow—*but don't steal*—there's always a good deal out there!

The Laning Chateau

When I first came to Palo Alto, I saw this grand eight-story building, finished in 1929 right before the depression hit: the Laning Chateau. I never saw a more beautiful building in my life. It was a gothic Prussian Grand Hotel of 1900 Berlin style with a penthouse and a dome. I loved it at first sight. I said, "God, if I could ever own that building." The Laning Chateau is an apartment building with ground floor commercial offices. Actually, the ground floor had been parking for old cars like they were built in the 1920s. Not today's cars; the cars were skinny back then.

And I did finally buy it, but it was a strange path to get there. The year was 1968, which was a strange year anyway. I was making a lot of trips to Mexico, often to Puerto Vallarta. And while there I loved to stay at the El Dorado Hotel. It was really a neat hotel. It had only twelve rooms, but they were big rooms, and only three on each floor. The penthouse was really huge because it was kinda built out over the hotel. I think there were actually two penthouses on the top. They also had the hottest restaurant and bar in town, right on the beach in Los Muertos, or Beach of the Dead. (For you curious about the name, it was called Beach of the Dead because it was where Emiliano Zapata fought and defeated the *federales* (government forces) after a fierce battle.)

Anyway, I loved the El Dorado Hotel enough to make a deal with Guillermo Wolff and Salvador Escalante, two people I really got to know well from my years of staying there. It was their hotel, and Salvador was the manager. I became more than just a guest; we got to be pretty good friends. One day, Salvador asked me if I was looking for something to buy and might I be interested in the El Dorado.

I said, "Salvador, I'd love to. But first off, you've got to be a Mexican citizen to own here on the beach."

He said, "Si, si, Denny. I'm a Mexican citizen, born and raised in Acapulco, but there is a new law now for purchasing a property. The gringos are bringing lots of money into Mexico. Puerto Vallarta has only just sprung up since 1962-1963, and look at it now. Building going on everywhere and it's gringo money. The new law is that a resident can own 25%, and a foreigner can own 75% through a Mexican trust. Why don't you plan to buy it and we will be partners together. I'll operate it."

I said, "Okay you've got a deal." So we sat down and drew up a partnership agreement, shook hands on it, and went to the Banco de National Industrial de Guadalajara in Guaymas. Because this was a Mexican Trust and the bank was holding it for me, this was all super duper. The deal was made and we were buying it for $200,000. I was putting up $150,000, and Salvador was putting up $50,000. He would go through an attorney to get the contract set up, and I would fly back to Palo Alto to arrange finances on my end. When I returned with the money, we would have everything done.

"This is unbelievable," I was thinking to myself. "I'm buying a hotel in Mexico—and what a place! This is 1968, I'm 29 years old, and I'm putting together this great deal. This is my dream!" Although coming up with the $150,000 was a real chore, I did it, and got a cashier's check from Bank of America made out to Banco de National Industrial de Guadalajara.

Then, just as I was getting ready to take off for Mexico, I received a phone call from this British guy named Paul. I can't remember his last name, only that he was not a nice man.

"Ow, Dennis, this is Paul. I have a surprise for you. I've got a listing on the Laning Chateau in Palo Alto. I heard you always wanted it. The owner died and Jim Starr, who is also your dentist, bought it out of the estate and now he wants to sell it." He paused and then said, "This is probably too big a deal for you, but I thought I'd let you know anyway."

I asked how much he wanted for it.

"Ow, he's in it at $650,000 and he would sell it for $650,000."

I thought, "Oh my God! $650,000 is a bargain." I mean, here we're talking 45 units plus commercial space, plus the penthouse up on top. So I tried everything I could to come up with the money I needed. I presented an offer for the full price of $650,000. The property had an existing $300,000 loan on it, so I only had to come up with $350,000, and I had a cashier's check for $150,000. Taking over the loan left me short by $200,000. I was wondering how I could make up the difference, so I threw in an eleven-unit building I had in Palo Alto, a house in Palo Alto, and a house I had in Mountain View. Plus my new Buick Skylark convertible. All I had remaining was my gun collection and my airplane, and I certainly wasn't going to give up my airplane, that was for sure. Oh did I love that airplane.

"Ow love that, you young punk!" he said to my offer. I'll never forget that. Nobody ever called me a punk before.

"You think Dr. Starr is gonna take that? Not on your life. Why would he want this crap! As far as I'm concerned, all you've got is $150,000. You still owe the rest and we want cash. There's no reason why 11 units and a house . . ."

As I said, I didn't like the man, and so I interrupted him. "Paul, that's all I have. I haven't got anything else. I'm leaving at seven o'clock tomorrow morning for Puerto Vallarta and taking this cashier's check with me. If I don't hear from you by seven o'clock about the offer I've made with all my assets, I'm going to buy the El Dorado Hotel. I'm offering you everything I have, including my Buick convertible."

"Ow you, not a chance. Who would want to deal with you?"

"The only place you could possibly reach me tomorrow is at the Playa de Cortez Hotel, but only if you call by six o'clock at night because that's when they shut down the switchboard. No calls in or out after that."

I left at seven o'clock in the morning, and I had with me the lovely Ellie Trout. What a gorgeous woman! Regrettably, Ellie had the personality of a dial tone. What is the personality of a dial tone? Well, this particular dial tone was bitch, bitch, bitch. She was never happy. She had to have her hair perfect, had to have her clothes perfect, had to stay in the most elegant places. The Playa de Cortez in Guaymas was a pretty good hotel. It was built in the 1930s and was a Southern Pacific Railroad Hotel. Really elegant.

I also had Jack and Mitzi Moynahan with me. I liked Mitzi; she was a good gal. Our first stop was going to be the fabulous Guaymas and we were off. Somehow, I had managed to totally forget about the Laning Chateau. It was behind me. I had my check and I was going to Puerto Vallarta to buy a fabulous hotel there and everything was an adventure.

We were flying down the Sea of Cortez passing Isla of Tiburon and coming up on Carlos Bay where I would make a left into the landing strip of Guaymas. As I was looking down, all of a sudden, I saw a brand new landing strip right on the edge of the beach. I wondered why would they put a landing strip right on the edge of the most gorgeous beach you ever saw.

I recalled that the newsletter from the Aircraft Owners and Pilots Association mentioned that Guaymas was getting a new hard surface strip, replacing its gravel strip. I was wondering, is this it? Why would they put the Guaymas strip way out here since this was San Carlos, not Guaymas? Guaymas was some 20 miles away. As I got lower, I was really startled to see, parked off the runway, a dozen B-25 Billy Mitchell bombers, and they all had American markings on the side. And not U.S.A., but U.S. Army Air Force Brown Devils, so they were pre-1943.

This was the weirdest thing I'd ever seen. I thought well, what the hell. We'll find out soon enough. I was flying final landing to the runway when all of a sudden, here I am maybe 250 feet off the ground just coming up on the approach, and there is an army jeep coming down the airstrip with a guy standing in the back waving red flags, waving me off from landing. I was thinking, what is this some sort of a clandestine base? What is going on? So I peeled off and headed to Guaymas.

Now the airfield at Guaymas was a small box with a gravel runway. Flying in there, we always tried to avoid getting rocks kicking up and making big dents in our fuselage. I knew this plane so well, I would hold it about a foot and a half off the ground, giving it enough power to just keep it flying until I would come up to the turn-off which, believe it or not, was asphalt. And I would just kinda turn the plane, side sweep it a bit, and boom, I'd sit it down on the asphalt turn-off. Maybe I would hit the gravel, then the turn-off, but I'd minimize the rock damage.

I always got a big welcome when I landed at Guaymas from Comandante Pacheco, who ran the airport, and then Fredrico, who was my taxi driver. Fredrico was always there waiting for me because I would call the La Playa de Cortez the day before and have Fredrico arrive about such and such a time. These were two great guys.

And so I got this big welcome. I helped Miss Personality out of her front seat, and then I got Jack and Mitzi out of the back seats. I said, "Well, everyone! Here you are in Mexico. Here you are in wonderful Guaymas, Mexico." Then I asked Comandante Pacheco and Fredrico, "What's the new airstrip out there? And the Army Air Force Base?"

"Oh, Señor LeVett," said the Comandante, "that has been so much fun. They are making a movie." And he proceeded to tell us that they were filming *Catch-22* with Alan Arkin and Richard Benjamin and a whole cast of stars at San Carlos Bay, about 25 miles from Guaymas. We also learned that everybody in the movie was staying here at Playa de Cortez.

Well, we all got settled in our hotel, and then got spiffed up to go downstairs for cocktails at six o'clock. Jack and

Mitzi and I were downstairs, waiting for Ellie, and we saw Alan Arkin, Richard Benjamin, Paula Prentiss, Orson Welles, and Martin Balsam. I mean the place was filled with famous faces. It was a real treat. Ellie wasn't there yet. Her hair had to be just perfect. An hour went by, Ellie still wasn't there yet. There were no phones in the room, so we sat at the bar drinking Margaritas, and eating giant shrimp, enjoying ourselves.

I heard Martin Balsam talking about "another stupid pilot from the United States thinking we're an airport where you can land. How many of these have we seen already?" He said, "This guy today was almost down on the runway. There was no stopping him. He was going to land there no matter what, and he ruined a scene." Then he went on to talk about the scene.

I knew exactly what he was talking about, of course. They were shooting that scene at the time I was coming in to land. So I said, "Excuse me, I was the stupid gringo pilot. I really apologize. There were no billboards, no media news broadcasts or anything else that announced they were making a movie here. Please, we won't bother you again. No flying low, no passes over your landing strip, no strafing."

He got a bit of a laugh out of that, and I said, "I feel very bad about this. I'd like to buy everybody a round of drinks, please." And that's just what I did. It was rather exciting for me. And soon we were all friends and yucking it up. Then Ellie finally came in. Everybody looked at Ellie because she was such a gorgeous brunette. Wow! She was a star in her own right, at least in terms of looks.

I think it was about ten o'clock that night when Fernando, the hotel manager, came into the restaurant and said, "Señor LeVett, we have an emergency telephone call for you." I said I didn't think there were any telephones.

He said, "The Gandara Hotel in Hermosillo owns us and they have a direct line to us, so this being an emergency, they got through."

Of course, it was Paul. He said, "I finally got to you,

punk! I've been trying for four hours to get a hold of you. This has been horseshit. Get back up here, right now! We need your deposit—you just bought the Laning Chateau."

I thought, "Oh my God! I don't believe I bought the Laning Chateau."

"I want you back here right away to open escrow, so we can get this thing going."

I said, "Hey, I'm on a vacation down here."

"You want it, or don't want it? You get up here by Monday!"

"Okay, Paul," I said. "You've got a deal! I'll be back to California with the cashier's check in the amount of $150,000 on Monday."

I sat there in shock. Absolute shock. There was no way of getting a phone call out to Puerto Vallarta to reach Salvador about the El Dorado deal. I regretted that, but life takes some strange turns, especially when you least expect them.

Anyway, the next day, Saturday, we all went out to San Carlos Bay to visit the movie set and then spent the rest of the day in Guaymas having a great time. The next day was Sunday and I decided I had to go home to close the deal on the Laning Chateau. This displeased my passengers, to say the least, because everybody was looking forward to going to Puerto Vallarta. So I decided to fly from where we were in Guaymas, on the mainland over to Mulege, which was in Baja California. I didn't like flying over the Sea of Cortez because it is loaded with sharks, but I kinda hop-scotched over islands on my chart and we made it safely; as safe as a landing can be at Mulege. We fueled up, and then flew up to Punta Chivato where we had a great lunch right by the pool at the new Punta Chivato Hotel. It sat right on the cliff overlooking the Sea of Cortez and was really an elegant place.

At cocktail hour, Ellie had a couple of drinks and we were all living it up. But then she disappeared. She was a moody girl. We talked to the hotel people, we talked to everybody. We were concerned because this was an area in those days that still had *bandito* problems, even though it was not on the mainland but over in Baja. Perhaps a more realistic concern was that there were a lot of wild animals — coyotes for sure, and mountain lions. People were warned not to go walking around the premises at night. They had this beautiful big swimming pool, but it was fenced off and guarded. So we all went out searching for Ellie. Finally we saw her darting from behind one tree to another. We were yelling at her, "Ellie, it's dangerous out here. There are wild animals."

Finally, Ellie gave up her game and came in, with the snottiest of attitudes. Looks are only skin deep, and this girl was all skin. I think after a few drinks she thought she'd have some fun trying to scare us; like she was thinking *they won't be able to find me and they'll get worried*. Yeah, right, we were worried! I didn't need to be hauling a body back up to Palo Alto. Anyway, we finally got Ellie under control and we all had dinner together. It was one of those beautiful nights, but we had to leave the next morning.

I had filled up in Mulege, which meant I'd used a half-hour of fuel. I pre-flighted the plane, checking the fuel and the rocker arm in front of the nose wheel under the carburetors that controlled the fuel with my little test tube jobby. Then we took off and I discovered that we had a helluva headwind. Over 40 knots coming against us, and that made fuel an issue. We had just passed over San Felipe, and I'm watching the fuel gauges bouncing off empty. They'd hit the redline — boom — and then go back up a little bit.

I had an hour flight left to Mexicali or I could go to Tijuana, but it wouldn't be any faster. Both were too far away with the fuel and the headwinds. I had to do something, so I got out my Mexico aviation handbook and saw that at San Felipe there was fuel at the back of a motel. (No kidding. Flying in Mexico could be a real challenge.)

The handbook stated that there were U.S. Army Air

Force 50-gallon drums behind the motel, and that attendants would pump fuel out for you, bring it to the airplane and run it through chamois to clean it. I was thinking, "Oh my God! But I don't have a choice." So I flew back around to San Felipe. It was then that I realized that I had read something about San Felipe Airport being flooded out. Soon I was flying over it, and sure enough, half of the runway was gone! Not one end or another but the center of the runway. A flash flood had come down the river and tore out half of the runway. The asphalt was gone. There was a gouge in the earth where the river had poured through.

I brought the plane in with full flaps, putting it just past the edge of the crevice. Boy, was I lucky! At the end of the runway was the road to town, so I just continued taxiing, right out onto the road. Thank God, there were no cars. People were watching me as I taxied down the road to the town of San Felipe.

I pulled up to the motel, and there at the back were dark green 50-gallon drums. On the side of the drums, it was marked *U.S. Army Air Force*. Of course, the people at the motel had no doubt why I was there. They brought a ladder out, pumped the gas into big cans and handed them up the ladder where a guy filled the tanks. Through a chamois (to use as a filter), I made sure.

While all that was going on, I was trying to figure out what in the hell had happened? Even with a headwind I shouldn't have been out of gas so that I was forced down in San Felipe. I tested the little rocker arm and discovered that when I pushed it, it stuck and there was a constant stream of fuel running out of it. I clicked the rocker arm back to where it was supposed to be. Whew! Was that a lesson. Don't be in too much of a hurry, I told myself. That could have cost me my life if I hadn't decided to turn around and fuel up at San Felipe.

(A note for non-pilots about fuel gauges. As the saying goes, they are right only twice: when they are full and when they are empty. Otherwise you can't rely on them to tell you how much fuel you have. You have to know your plane and how much fuel she uses per hour. And always . . . always leave yourself at least a half-hour of extra flying time, because maybe you'd hit a headwind, or have miscalculated or the engine was running richer, using more fuel, than you thought.)

Anyway, we got all fueled up, and it was time to go. We taxied back to the airport, took off into a good headwind, and made it home. No, I never saw Ellie again. Yes, I bought the Laning Chateau for $650,000, one of the best deals I ever made in my life. I sold it in the early teens of 2020, but it's worth over $15 million today. And it's the best looking building in Palo Alto.

I stayed close friends with Salvador Escalante. It was a good thing that I didn't buy into the El Dorado Hotel in Puerto Vallarta because a few years later, around 1976, President Echeverria was confiscating airplanes everywhere.

And there was another reason why the Puerto Vallarta deal wouldn't have worked. Salvador told me, "Denny, everybody's getting sick from the water down here. Everybody's sick from the food. We can't get the federal government to spend money. That Echeverria, he only spends on terrorism. We need a water system, we need everything. It's tough on tourism. My employees, they're stealing me blind. There are strikes every other week." And he said, "You're so lucky you didn't buy into this."

A postscript to this story. Maybe it's that time heals all wounds. When Echeverria was finally out of power, the El Dorado got a new lease on life. The owners turned it into condominiums, a really great setup, but they kept the bar and restaurant, which was still the hottest place in town. Oh, it was pretty. But I never had any regrets about nixing the El Dorado deal for the Laning Chateau. I made the right decision. No question.

Giving the Customers What They Want

It was when I took over the Benbow Inn that I first realized the value of a dog friendly hotel. My white poodle, Jacques, went with me everywhere, and I just naturally wanted him to stay with me at the Benbow. This was what led me to consider the prospect of a dog-friendly hotel. Initially, I worried about the rugs and bedding—but then, I thought "why not?" It occurred to me that people are much happier traveling with their dogs. "Why haven't hotels thought of this before"? I wondered to myself. We should switch things around—leave the children at home and bring the pets!" And so, the Benbow Inn became a dog-friendly hotel under my ownership.

When I first purchased the Benbow, our dining room, which held 107 people, served only about 75 dinners a night during the prime tourist season. I sat down with my chef and I said, "Okay. We're only selling 75 dinners a night and no locals are coming for dinner. Why don't the locals come here?"

"It's pretty expensive," he replied. "And Mr. Stadler, the former owner, didn't want local people here. He thought they would be troublemakers in the bar."

I said, "Okay." It wasn't really okay, but what I meant was—what *else?*

"There are some other things you've got to understand, Mr. LeVett. We try not to sell . . . well, I mean, we need to have it on the menu, but we try not to sell the abalone. We try not to sell the lobster tail and the Lobster Mornay, and we try not to sell the Beef Wellington and the baseball-cut sirloins and the New York strips."

"Why do we try not to sell them?" I asked.

"Because our food cost on those dishes are over 55 to 60

percent of the prices."

"Wait a minute. We're not selling these items because the food costs are too high?"

"Absolutely."

"So what are we selling?"

He said, "Well, we want to sell the lamb, because we buy the lamb for next to nothing. We get all our lamb from Shilo, so we can sell that dinner for 6.95 or 7.50—and it's a full dinner." *(This is back in 1974. Prices were, um, lower back then.)*

He continued, "Then, of course, the fish. We get the Red Snapper, the Petrale Sole, and the Rock Cod brought down fresh out of Eureka. We send Roy over to Shelter Cove every day. At Shelter Cove, we get the day boat salmon, and we can sell a full salmon dinner for $7.50. Our food costs are down below 50 percent on those items. It just works for us. It works for us beautifully. Also, the chicken that we sell is profitable."

"How much do we charge for Beef Wellington?" I asked.

"Beef Wellington is $25 a meal, and the sirloins, the baseball cut, that's $19.50. And the abalone and the Lobster Mornay, we sell for that for $25 a meal."

I said, "Jeff, starting right now, we sell every Lobster Mornay, every Beef Wellington, every abalone, in fact, everything we can get." I asked him, "What do we make with all our special items, the salmon, the petrale sole, the lamb, the snapper, the chicken—do we make $5?"

"No, we don't make $5," he answered.

"You're right. We make about $3 a dinner when we could be making $10 or $15 a dinner. Forget Stadler's food costs theory. Sell what I tell you to sell!"

So, from then on, we went from 75 dinners a night to 175 dinners a night. I spoke to a lot of wealthy people in the area and we got them eating in our dining room—the bankers, the men who owned the car dealerships, the ranchers, and the lumber tycoons. They all began coming to the Benbow Inn for dinner, some of them several times a week.

All of a sudden, the Benbow Inn in the summertime, well, it wasn't unusual to do 250 dinners a night. And just as all of a sudden, the bank account at Bank of Eureka, Charlie Shriner's bank, shot up—boom! It was like a veritable slot machine, but with winners every time. The moral of the story here is that sometimes you have to spend money in order to make money—and most importantly, never disregard *any* customer group in your market, especially the locals.

We gave them what they wanted, and in doing so, we pleased everyone . . . which is exactly what we aim to do at the Cypress Inn for the people of Carmel. Read on.

The Vagabond's House Inn

The Vagabond's House Inn, in Carmel by the Sea, was not only renowned as one of the four finest inns on the West Coast, it also had one of the highest occupancy rates of any lodging in the country.

As I mentioned previously, it just so happened that one Saturday my friend Barbara needed to be on the Monterey Peninsula to take her scuba diving certification test on Monastery Beach in Carmel. So I phoned Chuck Watts, the owner of the Vagabond's House, who had invited me down to stay at his inn a number of times, and asked him if we could drive to Carmel and stay for Friday and Saturday night.

I didn't know much about the Vagabond's House except that it was small, but highly respected and successful. I also learned that Chuck was a master at that front desk. He kept that place full. And he would never take a Friday/Saturday reservation. People had to take Friday, Saturday, and Sunday.

Chuck said to me, "Denny, I am so sorry, we are full."

I found that hard to believe and said, "Chuck, this is December 10th."

"Denny, we're full. I'm awfully sorry. You've got to come some other time."

I persisted, "I can't believe you're full." And what really made this so strange, aside from the unlikelihood that they would be booked this time of year, was that Watts had been after me for years to sell the Benbow Inn to him.

"Yeah," he said, "we're full all the time. Please call me again. We'd love to have you stay here with us. You'd love Vagabond's House Inn. So sorry, Denny."

I was just hanging up when I heard a voice in the

background. It was his wife Patsy, "Chuck, you dumb son of a bitch." Then click. It was only thirty seconds later when the phone rang.

"Denny, This is Chuck. We just had a cancellation. I've got a room for you."

Well, thanks to Patsy, I did stay at Vagabond's House that weekend and I fell in love with it. In fact, I still love it, to this day. I ended up bartering the Vagabond's House Inn as part of the down payment when Chuck bought the Benbow Inn from me. The Benbow featured 72 rooms, plus a formal dining room and a bar, and it sat right on the edge of the Eel River with its beautiful beaches. At the time, the Benbow was worth a helluva lot more than Vagabond's House. Not today, though. Tourism's way down up there in Garberville, and way up in Carmel.

In six months, that deal was done, and Chuck went up North to apprentice at the Benbow. I sent Jewel Brown, my trusted Mrs. Brown who'd been running the Benbow, down to Carmel to run Vagabond's House. She was the greatest innkeeper that ever lived. She won a whole slew of awards for being the world's consummate innkeeper. When I finally got down to Carmel and checked our occupancy rate, I learned that we were full, full, full. Mrs. Brown, who didn't always have the time to make deposits, had drawers full of money. Unbelievable.

Buying the Cypress Inn

There was a time in the mid-Eighties when the Pine Inn in Carmel by-the-Sea came up for sale. I already had a number of lodging properties in Carmel at the time, and I made a pass at the Pine Inn for ten million. I think it sold to a guy from Fresno for twelve million. Then I heard that the Cypress Inn on Lincoln & 7th was available, so I called Lou F. who was the attorney representing the owner. I'd known Lou and always thought of him as a good guy.

"Okay, Lou," I said. "I'll pay full price. You were asking four million, I'll pay four million."

"Good," he said.

"How do you want it?" I asked. "Do you want it all in cash, or do you want to have me carry back, or do you want to carry back the deed of trust, with your savings on taxes, of course. Just tell me how you want it."

"Fine, Denny I'll get back to you in the next couple of days."

"We've got a deal?"

"We've got a deal," he said.

I repeated, "We've got a deal. Have I bought it?"

He said something like, "I don't see any reason why you haven't. Yes, you've done it."

Anyway, a couple of days went by, and I called Lou's office, and he said, "Den, they sold the Inn."

I was so disappointed. Furious would be a better word. Then I got a phone call from Dick Albers, another real estate investor from Palo Alto that I'd known for a number of years. Albers said, "Denny, I have this group, four of us, and we have bought Cypress Inn.

I said, "I don't believe it. I thought *I* bought the Cypress Inn."

He said, "No, we got a contract."

"How the hell did you get a contract?"

"Lou. We told him we were buying it. We've got until noon tomorrow to remove the contingencies."

"What do you mean, 'remove the contingencies?'"

He said, "Well, we're going to bring in partners. We have these guys who own the Mission Ranch—they are trying to sell Mission Ranch—who will come in. They'll all come in for a certain amount."

That sounded somewhat odd to me, and I asked, "Okay. Why do you want me?"

"Well," Albers said, "you're somebody who has a hotel background who can run the thing and be a partner. David Wolfe will be the general manager."

I could make the story go on for really a whole book, but you don't need to know all of the back-n'-forth, because frankly, it was pretty mixed up. Anyway, I called Lou F. and we had a civilized conversation. I said, "Lou, I'm very disappointed. I thought I had the deal. I wanted the hotel. I can't believe you had any doubts that I could raise the money. Money is not a problem."

He said, "Well, they bought it, and it seemed like the right thing, and I know the guys. They have a whole group, and its the group that owns Mission Ranch."

Without telling him that I already knew, I said, "The group that owns Mission Ranch, they've been trying to make condos out of it. They're doing everything the wrong way, and they're going to have to sell Mission Ranch to have the money to buy the Cypress."

I told Lou, "This Albers group, they said they wouldn't move forward and buy it, unless I'd go in with them. They wanted a hotel guy to go in with them." Then I said, "So Lou, if this deal falls through, I'll take it. I'll buy it. Will you sell it to me if they can't pull it together?"

"Denny, I'm sorry I can't, because there's already two backup offers."

I want to tell you, I was angrier than I can remember. I

knew Lou. I'd done business with him. He knew I wanted the Cypress, and he was giving everyone else first choice over me. So, I called Albers and said, "Okay, I'll go in, but I want a third and I'll be general partner." I wasn't happy with the deal because I didn't want to do this partnership, but if I didn't do the partnership, I'd never be able to have the Cypress Inn.

We went ahead and at the close of escrow, there was only 20% for me, not the third I said I wanted. I had a big fight with Dick Albers and Duesenberry, one of the others who was also in the Mission Ranch deal. Albers said, "Well, you brought some of your guys in. You brought in the Wild Turkeys (a group of my friends), and you brought in John Hanna (another friend), and so you don't get as much because we had our guys." Well, it was a dumb-ass bad deal, but I bit my lip and we closed escrow.

I operated the Cypress, and the taste in my mouth got worse as I had to deal with my partners. These guys were impossible to work with. Absolutely nitpicky. They would come down to Carmel and demand free rooms and free food, eating into profits, as if it was their private club and not a money-making business. I told them they didn't know a thing about the hotel business, and that they were also running the Mission Ranch into the ground. I told them to stop treating me like an employee and to take a look at the ownership. I reminded them that I was the boss and the general partner, and that what I say, goes.

I really began to dislike these guys, and a couple of them I've known all my life and throughout my career in Palo Alto. So, I contacted each of the partners and I said, "I'll buy you all out for cash and give you all the profit."

Everyone agreed, but then Dick Albers nixed it, "No, it's worth more than that. No, you can't do that." A number of the partners followed his lead and wanted their money back. I wanted out of this partnership so badly. Jesus, I didn't like anybody involved. So, those who wanted to get their money back, I gave them their money back. A bunch of them didn't want their money back, they wanted to go ahead. It was a mess. I just couldn't wait to get out of the partnership. I didn't know how I was going to do it.

While I was aching to get out of the partnership, at the same time, I really didn't want to lose the Cypress Inn. I was running it every day. I don't think I've ever had a situation like that in my life, where I felt like I didn't do anything wrong; it was all the other guys. Except that I should have somehow, someway, gotten to Lou sooner and closed that deal before anybody else did. I just felt helpless.

Well, it took some time, some patience, and some wrangling, but eventually, in 1986, I managed to buy out the other partners, and I must say that they all made a very good gain—every single one of those guys netted a $100,000 profit over two years. It was after this experience, that I swore never to have another partnership again. But *never say never*, as the saying goes, because fate was about to walk through the door . . .

*   *   *   *   *

. . . When she was three, my daughter Amanda attended pre-school at the Santa Catalina School in Monterey. Her mother would take her there every morning. Terry Melcher's son, Ryan, was also going to the same pre-school. So Amanda, being a tomboy, and Ryan, a wonderful little thug, hit it off as pretty good friends. Ryan was a mischievous boy. Amanda was kinda a mischievous girl. And in those days I was flying up to Palo Alto to my office there, where I would spend four days a week, maximum. Sometimes, I went for two days and then back, depending upon whether there was a big social function or what have you. This was when I was doing all my own flying.

At the time I was flying a 182, a 175 part of the time, and a Hawk XP. (I really liked that airplane.) It was over a period of some twenty years that I commuted by plane to Palo Alto, probably twice if not three times a week. In fact, it got so that

I was daily commuting up until about 10 years ago. I always felt that I had to be there on Friday afternoon to finish up the week.

The whole week would just come to a climax at about five o'clock in Palo Alto. The routine was that I'd check the airplane out, and take the proverbial bird's nests out of the cowling, and then fly down to Monterey. It was a short flight, but there was frequently fog and I got awfully good at sneaking in the back door. That meant flying around or under the fog so I didn't have to fly by instruments, which I really hated because it involved paying too much attention to the instruments and not enjoying the flight. I would try to come down the Salinas Valley and then follow Highway 68 under the fog to the airport. The highway was like an extended flight path that took me right to the runway.

I think maybe once or twice I landed in Salinas, but I almost always got in. Of course, I was smart enough to call ahead to check and see how the fog was. There were a number of times that I had to hop in the car and drive down because the pea soup was thick at both airports. I much preferred to fly, especially with the weekend traffic on Fridays. Karen, my wife at the time, would pick me up at the airport. I'd come home, have a vodka martini, sit back, play with the dogs and the kids, and have a happy Friday night. Once in a while we'd go out, but I tried not to.

But, this one particular Friday night, Karen called me and said, "Denny, we're going out to dinner tonight . . .

Doris Day

"Happy Anniversary, Doris!"
"Anniversary?" she said.
"Doris, do you know we've been business partners for 32 years?"
There was a kind of muffled sound and then she gasped, "Denny, my goodness, that's the longest relationship I've had with any man!"

So, let me tell you the story of how I met Doris Day . . .

On that fateful Friday night in 1987, when my wife Karen called me and said, "Denny, we're going to dinner with Terry and Jacqueline Melcher tonight," I asked, "Who are Terry and Jacqueline Melcher?"

"Well you know. That's Doris Day's son and his wife. They're Ryan's mother and father." Ryan was my daughter Amanda's best friend at the Santa Catalina School in Monterey.

Our local hangout in those days was the Rio Grill. Bill Cox, the owner, was one of my best friends. As it turned out, I really enjoyed chatting with Terry. He was a true wit, and we were both hitting it off. I was making him laugh, and he was making me laugh. His stories about old Hollywood and the Beach Boys, who he managed for many years, and the like, were fascinating.

Then he said, "Karen tells me you're in the hotel business."

I said, "Yeah. Have been for quite a while." We talked about the Benbow Inn that I owned in Garberville, and the Vagabond's House Inn in Carmel.

He said, "My mom and I tried to buy a bunch of hotels. Bud Allen was going to sell the Sundial, and we made a deal with him one night at a party to buy it for $4 million. But, we all partied hard in those days and Bud would forget about it by the next day. We thought we'd bought it from him a couple of times, but the same scenario always played out."

"Terry, isn't that funny?" I said. "I thought I bought it from Bud too. I'd call him the next day and he'd totally forgotten about the conversation the night before. I think he really didn't want to sell."

Terry added that they once tried to buy the Pine Inn, and I told him that I had attempted to buy it, too.

"The one that mom and I really wanted," he said, "was the Cypress Inn. But there were so many buyers out there, and by the time we got around to it, it had already been sold."

He continued to say he'd heard there were problems with the partnership at the Cypress Inn, and that the general partner really wanted to sell out. He asked if I would be interested in talking to his mom and him about buying into it with them, because I had a hotel background and he understood that I was a pretty good businessman, according to Bud Allen. He thought I might be interested in buying out the general partner and then we could buy the limited partners out.

I said, "Frankly, Terry, we're halfway there because I *was* that general partner. That'd be me!"

He'd had no idea. "And let me update you," I said. "I *did* get out of that deal and bought out the rest of the partners. I am the sole owner of the Cypress Inn. I didn't want to get out of the hotel, I wanted to get out of the partnership, and I did whatever it took to accomplish that."

As a result of that most fateful Friday night dinner, Doris Day and Terry and I met several times and all got along very well. I liked her very much, and I think she liked me because, in 1987, we made an agreement to co-own the Cypress Inn. Although I swore never to make a partnership deal again, the long and short of it was that I thought it was a great idea to have Doris as my partner. Doris Day helped put the Cypress Inn on the map. Her one condition was that the 44-room hotel remain dog friendly. "I only like hotels that allow dogs," she told me.

I don't mean to sound arrogant in any way, but I always considered the Cypress Inn to be so much more than an old hotel. When I first saw it, back in the late '50s, I was immediately struck by how beautiful it was. I had always gravitated to grand old hotels, back from those early trips to Europe in my youth. And to me, this was the picture of elegance. And that front doorway! I made that front door our logo because it was something I remembered from the first time I saw that place. I thought it was an elegant private club when I first saw it.

The Cypress Inn was always special. It not only has great architecture and great location, but is a hub of activity in Carmel-by-the-Sea. In the early days, they did have a restaurant, but the bar wasn't there. In fact, where the front bar is now, now known as the Dog Bar where "Yappy Hour" occurs, was formerly the registration desk where you checked in. So I moved the check-in desk up front, where it always should have been, and then added the food and drinks bar. Immediately, it became everyone's favorite little bar in town because it had the patio and beautiful scenery, along with Doris Day posters decking the walls. We also offered live music in the salon that became very popular with both tourists and locals alike.

But the big secret of the Cypress Inn is the dogs! Of course, I always wanted to create a happy, homey place, but the beauty of having pets present is that people will see a dog and compliment the owner and before you know it, they have struck up a conversation. You never know who you might meet at Yappy Hour. This is how friendships begin. We've seen it time and again, fellow dog lovers agreeing "Same place, same time next year?" And there you've got an annual tradition.

I later expanded the Cypress, buying the property next door, putting in suites, a dining room and a big bar. It's one of those things in life that all kinda worked; it all came together. I made it very clear to the whole staff that locals were number one; that we paid attention and cultivated the locals, no matter what. And oh, did that pay off! The locals, and the dogs, made that place what it is.

Now we have wonderful music in the living room and we attract locals, as well as pleasing the out of town guests. People who are staying at other lodging come here for dinner, to sit on the patio, to listen to the music. Where else can you find that? Where else can you find that feeling?

I've also put my old toy airplanes and toy soldiers in display cases at the Cypress Inn. I know some people think it's curious for a grown up to be interested in toy soldiers, but I've been collecting them all my life. When I got my first soldiers, they sold for five cents at Woolworth's and Ben Franklin stores. They came from England through Canada. Up in Canada you could buy them at Fort Williams and Port Arthur for 10 cents apiece. I enjoyed placing the soldiers and re-enacting famous battles. Now, I just collect them, and am constantly on the hunt. I sometimes find them in antique stores, and today, I have a significant collection. The Cypress Inn is a stage for me in a way, and I just love it. In truth, the Cypress is the most special thing in my life, after my wife, my daughters, my grandson, my poodles, and my friends, of course.

Yes, it all turned out just the way I wanted it to. Today, "Terry's Lounge" is named after Doris Day's son Terry, who passed away in 2004. I have so many heartwarming memories of Doris and Terry together at his baby grand piano. Terry would play and sing Christmas carols. Doris would listen to the first one, hum the second one, and sing the third one, and then each one afterwards. It was unbelievable to witness, as Doris had pretty much given up singing publicly, by the time I knew her.

I will also cherish the memory of having attended the 1989 Golden Globe Awards ceremony in Beverly Hills when Clint Eastwood presented Doris Day with the Cecil B. DeMille Award. And did she ever deserve it!

Doris was a very private person and kept a low profile, but she did attend a celebration of her 90th birthday at the Cypress Inn, and would occasionally come for dinner, served in a secluded room upstairs in Terry's Lounge. I recall she liked the Sand Dabs.

The most frequent question I'd be asked at the Cypress Inn was, "How old is Doris Day?" And you could understand it, because there are movie posters all over the walls of the lobby showing a young Doris Day at the height of her acting career.

So several years back, while I was visiting at her home, I came right out and asked her about this most common question. I said, "Doris, I always thought you were 87, not 89 (at that time). I think I'm right, aren't I?"

She answered, "You sure are, Dennis. You sure are."

Here's why there was some confusion about her age. Doris Day started her singing career when she was just 16 years old. But because, at that time, it was against the law to sing professionally until you were 18, she had to tell everyone that's how old she was. Also, because she posed for many photographs during that time, the fan magazines went along with those two extra years on her age by calling her 18, without checking any further. This never bothered her until about 5 or 6 years before her death when she felt it would be better to tell her real age, which was two years younger than the magazines printed. So, in 2018, it was revealed that she was actually 94. And, let me add, she looked great. Not *still* great—but just as great as she always has.

I thought Doris Day would live to be 100, but on May 13, 2019, she passed away at 97 years of age at her beloved home in Carmel Valley. She really was the best. In all our years of working together, we never had one argument, not one misunderstanding. It was heaven.

I grew up in Iowa as a farm boy, and my dream was to someday find a girl just like Doris Day. I'd never have guessed that one day I'd be in business with her. It was the best partnership — and the most fun, I've ever had.

*   *   *   *   *

There is a postscript to this story. About two months after I started negotiations with the limited partners to buy out the Cypress Inn, Doug Schmitz, who was the Carmel City Administrator, approached me to purchase the Mission Ranch. "These guys are going to make a mess of it. They want to subdivide it. They want to do condominiums down there. It can be bought for four million."

What a coincidence, I thought.

"Would you please buy it?" Doug said, "We'll give you what you want." He went into great detail about it. You want so many units, et cetera, et cetera.

"We'll do that for you. We'll give that to you, but we need an owner we can work with. We've worked with you on the Gambel property and at several other properties, with you and Chris Tescher. We've been very happy, so will you buy it?"

I said, "Well, okay, I'll try to buy it."

I think it was during this time when the negotiations over the purchase of the Cypress Inn were taking place that Clint Eastwood became Mayor of Carmel. Not long thereafter, Doug Schmitz came back and said, "Denny, I'm sorry to do this. You're ready to close escrow on the Mission Ranch, but would you mind if Clint Eastwood took over the escrow?"

I didn't want to tell Doug that I had my hands full and that this was the biggest favor he could have done for me. Anyway I said, "Okay," feigning disappointment, "For Eastwood, I'll do this." The fact was that I didn't have an extra four million in hand at that time that I could borrow. And that's how Clint Eastwood got the Mission Ranch.

The Trip to the Hudson River Valley

By 1978, I had sold the BenBow Inn and had taken over the Vagabond's House Inn. Vagabond's House was one of the four best inns on the West Coast. Of those four inns, I owned two of them, though not at the same time. This was according to Norm Simpson, who called himself the *Berkshire Traveler*; yes, he lived in the Berkshires. He was famous for his *Country Inns and Back Roads* guidebook. (I visited Norm a number of times in Stockbridge, Massachusetts where he was also a friend of Norman Rockwell. I stayed at the Red Lion when I visited him. Regrettably, he was paralyzed in an automobile accident, and he eventually took his own life. But what a pal!)

It was 1981, and I was in Carmel. My wife's best friends were Joyanne and Aram Kenosian. They always stayed at the spiffiest, best hotels. We were planning a trip to go back and visit Norm Simpson. He was setting us up with the most famous inns on the East Coast, so we flew into New York, where he had booked us for a stay at the Algonquin Hotel. It was charming as hell. Joyanne and Aram, and my wife hated it. They always stayed at the Plaza or the Pierre, their favorites.

Then we drove up the Hudson and went through Sleepy Hollow. We drove to Starlight Lake, which was in Pennsylvania, just across the New York border. Denise, who worked for me, had arranged for us to stay at what was supposed to be this spectacular inn at Starlight Lake. Her uncle and aunt owned the place. But when we arrived, our faces just dropped. The place was hippy-ville. Not cool. Not elegant. Not what we thought it was supposed to be. All the rooms had that fake, quarter-inch thin wood veneer paneling.

Joyanne wouldn't sleep without her clothes on. It was the worst inn I've ever stayed at. All night long, the moose (this place was famous for moose) were mating. You could hear their honking all night long. They didn't sleep, I didn't sleep. We couldn't wait to get out of there in the morning. Joyanne and Aram were so mad at me. They had expected a more luxurious vacation, and had brought so much luggage that the car—a good size Buick—was so weighted down that it was only a few inches off the ground.

What I didn't learn until I got to Stockbridge and saw Norm Simpson was that he would never have sent me to Starlight Lake—ever. In fact, he wanted to take Starlight Lake out of his book because it just didn't live up to his standards.

I had a stern conversation with Denise when I returned. I said, "I don't care if you're proud of your aunt and uncle. You shouldn't have done that, Denise." She knew the difference, for goodness sakes.

Misplaced Trust

It's been 52 years since I started my company, and it has been pretty successful from Day One. I bought properties and did my own painting and plumbing. I had help, of course, but I picked the right buildings to invest in—apartment rentals and house rentals in Palo Alto. It's just been straight up the whole time. Not just in terms of being profitable, but also of maintaining the quality of the buildings, the upkeep and the administration.

Who would have guessed that Palo Alto would become the most sought after place to start a business, or go into business, or go to college, and become the Wall Street of Silicon Valley? It all happened—and is still happening—in Palo Alto.

Mostly I developed existing properties, but I also built apartment buildings, four different apartment buildings, and remodeled many, many more in Palo Alto. In Carmel and Pebble Beach, I built some spec houses. I did all those with Chris Tescher. He and I have been partners for over 40 years.

I've done well for myself in business over the years, but it hasn't all gone smoothly. Three incidents stand out. They were upsetting and costly, and I could have prevented at least two of them from happening, if . . . the *if*'s were if I had been playing closer attention and if I hadn't given my employees such loose reins.

The first situation was at the Cypress Inn, not long after I had taken control of the operation. There was a man, we'll call him Harold Spume, who had worked for me at the Vagabond's House Inn. I brought Harold over to the Cypress Inn because the first general manager we had there was inept, and Harold had done a pretty good job for me at Vagabond's House.

But Harold was in over his head at the larger, more complicated situation at the Cypress. He made some decisions without consulting me, and refused to follow my direct orders.

My mistakes were in not keeping a closer eye on what was going on, and in thinking that Harold just needed to pull himself together. For example, I told Harold to hire a chef for the restaurant, and to pay him no more than $80,000, which was a lot of money for our size restaurant over thirty-five years ago. I checked out the guy and found that he had good credentials, and maybe he was good for the places he worked. It's also possible that his previous employers were vouching for him so he wouldn't sue them if they told the truth.

The chef turned out to be a disaster. For instance, everybody who came into the restaurant wanted a hamburger. This was because there wasn't another good hamburger in the city of Carmel, but we had great hamburgers at the Cypress. This chef (should I call him Kooky?) would only allow four hamburgers to be served per night. This was because he wanted to encourage people to try other things. Then he added a $5 charge for splitting hamburgers. I was ready to kill Harold when I found out. I should have killed them both, but I don't even kill squirrels.

Anyway, it wasn't long after that, when I was out of the country, that I got a call in the middle of the night from a Cypress employee. He said, "You can't believe what's happened here. The chef has gone nuts. He won't let anybody season any of his food. He's going around with a hammer to every table and smashing every salt and pepper shaker."

I told Harold to fire the chef, that I was cutting short my trip and would soon be returning to Carmel. When I got back, I immediately got rid of Harold. I thought of suing him, but decided against it. Good riddance. I don't know what happened to Harold, but I confess that when I think back on that situation, I am disappointed mainly in myself for hiring him in the first place, and not overseeing him. It was my business. I was the owner. It was my responsibility.

Wheeler Bad Dealer

Chuck F. was a big, big-time wheeler-dealer. In fact, he did a couple of buildings in Carmel that are smashing, but he was the epitome of playing with other people's money. His big scheme was putting off the closing, having deposits set up with contingencies and not removing the contingencies because he kept finding out certain things. Sometimes, the delay in the closing would be so long that the seller became desperate and cut the price.

Chuck also had an improper practice in which he got five different banks to give him a loan to do major renovations on the same house; those loans being delivered and filed the same day, so none of the banks would know about the other loans.

I was smart enough to keep my distance from him, or at least, so I thought. I came to learn that Chuck had used my name a number of times with a couple of banks, saying, "Oh, I've done deals with Denny LeVett." Or "Denny LeVett will back me on these prices. Call Denny LeVett. He will give you his opinion." And it was without asking me. It got to the point, because he knew they were going to call me, that he did say, "Oh, by the way, I used your name, Denny. I hope that's okay." No, it wasn't, and I told him so in no uncertain terms.

It wasn't long before everybody was calling Chuck a bad dealer. Word had gotten out about his unscrupulous tactics, and the fact that everybody was after him. I was with a group of people coming back from skiing in Vail when his name came up. Someone said, "I'll bet he's down in Argentina."

My friend, Pete Blackstock said, "I think he's over in Australia and New Zealand, because he had some holdings or made some investments over there."

I said, "You guys, I'm going to tell you something, Chuck's favorite place in the world is the Cotswolds. He would always say, 'Someday I'm going to live in the Cotswolds.' That was his favorite place in the world. I'll bet he turns up in the Cotswolds. That might be where he is now."

"Well, you know, Denny," said one of the group, "there's a rumor about this redhead that's hanging around with him. He has been seen with this redhead, who is an admiral's daughter."

"Uh-oh," I said. "That's dangerous."

This story picks up later with Bill Tyler, a friend of mine from Palo Alto and Kansas City, who became very wealthy, bought a huge manor house built in the 16th century in Broadway, in the Cotswolds in England. He had it redone and updated, of course. Fabulous place.

Every time I would go to the Cotswolds, because I loved it there also, I went looking for property; in particular, looking for a couple of manor houses or a small hotel. This was when I sold the Benbow Inn. I was already thinking of buying a hotel, the Pioneer, in Carmel. My grand plan was to have a hotel in England, one in Hawaii, and one in Carmel.

One of Bill Tyler's best friends and mine was Bill Reller; Bill and I were in partners in the Laning Chateau in Palo Alto. Bill and Carolyn Reller had been over to see Bill Tyler in the Cotswolds. They had a great time.

When Bill Reller got back, he said, "Let's have lunch. I've got to tell you something."

He said over lunch, "You know Broadway. You've been looking for hotels over there." He showed me some pictures from his trip, including one of a big manor house owned by Bill Tyler's neighbor, who was standing in front of his house.

"Oh," he said. "You know him. You stayed with him."

I shook my head to disagree. "I've never seen him before in my life."

"Denny, boy, is he pissed off at you."

"How can he be pissed off at me, Bill? I don't even know him. I've never seen the man in my life."

"Well, yeah, you did, Denny. You stayed with him."

I got annoyed. "You know, Bill, in all the years we've known each other, if there is ever a question about, 'no, I haven't/yes, you have', I always lose because you always take the negative route. And for a close, close friend, I need to tell you, I'm a little tired of it. Now, I'm going to say it to you once more. I've never seen this guy in my life. I never stayed with him."

Bill said, "Well, further than that, you made a deal with him in writing and you bought his manor house to turn it into a hotel. And he's got your business card and everything else."

"He's got my business card and everything else? What in the hell are you talking about?"

"Well, you were trying to buy his hotel. And I know you told me in the past that you tried to buy a hotel in Broadway, and I assumed this was it. I mean, he wants to sue you."

"Bill, this is absolute nonsense," I said. "I need to get the description of this guy he is talking about." I didn't have to think about it. I knew right away. "I know who it is. Chuck is posing as me with Denny LeVett business cards."

I called Bill Tyler. "Bill, didn't it occur to you that if I was staying with your friend in Broadway at his manor house, that I would be coming to see you and Susanne who live half a mile away?"

"Well, yeah, it does seem that way, Denny."

"Can you get me a description or can you get me the number of this guy?"

"Tell you what," he promised. "I will call you back with a description." And he added, "Then you can talk to my friend yourself."

He called me back and said, "No. It sure wasn't you. I described you to him, how you talked, how you acted. It sure in the hell wasn't you. This guy looked nothing like you. He was tall and dark."

I said, "I know who it was. It was Chuck posing as me. The description fits."

The whole story began to come out, that Chuck showed up and he had my business card. Whether he printed them up or whether he got some from me over the years or what—he had my business card, posed as me owning hotels, and even had brochures of my hotels in Carmel, including the Cypress Inn. I was furious, but relieved that I could begin to clear my name in the Cotswolds.

Some months later, I heard that authorities had found Chuck at a posh restaurant in Monte Carlo and Interpol agents had arrested him. (Scuttlebutt had it that he had been cheating on the red-head who, out of spite, turned him into the authorities.) Chuck finally went to trial on charges of fraud and then to prison. He was sentenced to five to ten years in a "Club Fed" prison, but wound up spending only a fraction of the time behind bars.

But the story isn't over, because one day I got a phone call. It was Chuck himself. They had put him in a halfway house in Salinas. He called me one day and said, "Hey, I get out on Tuesday. How about having lunch?"

I replied, "Chuck, I'm tempted, really tempted, because I would really love to hear the story someday. But we would probably have some differences of opinion, like about the success you had posing as me in the Cotswolds, and who knows where else you posed as me."

"Pose as you?" he said. "I would not do that. I never have. Never even been in the Cotswolds. No, never."

I'd had it. "Chuck, thou protesteth too much." I felt a flashback to the memory of my anger when I first heard of his getting me into such a mess in the Cotswolds. I said, "You have to know that I don't like you. I don't want to have lunch with you. I don't want to sit down and talk to you. I know too much about you." End of discussion.

I saw him again because he still had his membership in

the Pebble Beach Club. He would come over and pretend we were friends. But the pretense wouldn't work. I'm a very forgiving person, but Chuck had gone too far.

Buying the Carmel Pine Cone

Yes, it's true, I was briefly (and only technically) the owner and publisher of the *Carmel Pine Cone* (the very popular local newspaper in Carmel, California). But boy, is that a convoluted story.

As it goes, there was a piece of property that I wanted to buy and develop with my builder-partner Chris Tescher. It sat on the edge of Pescadero Canyon, on the border between Pebble Beach and Carmel. Doug Schmitz, who was the City Manager of Carmel, was concerned about lawsuits against the city that would force it to have a subdivision of six houses on a mountainside in that area. He wanted me and Tescher to buy the whole piece and build two houses on the property.

We told the city we would go ahead and buy this big lot. We'd take this one big parcel and we'd make it into two lots, and then we could build two houses on the side of the canyon. Tescher went along with it because it was important to the city. So Doug Schmitz said, "Okay, you guys, we work well with you and we've done other projects with you, and we like Tescher/LeVett. We will give you two lots."

Okay. Good. So we bought the property. I think it was around 1989, if I remember correctly, and it was quite a bit of money—around $600,000.

Once we got the property, we had to take it before the Carmel City Council to get the approval to build the two houses. We were shocked when they turned us down. We went back to Doug and he said, "Hold on. They don't get it that you helped us out in this situation. We'll get you the two lots."

"Doug," I told him, "we've gotta have two lots there, otherwise the whole thing doesn't work."

He replied, "Well, you've got the lot over on the Pebble Beach side."

I informed him that there were problems on the Pebble Beach side, too—but in the meantime, I had lost faith in the Carmel City Council. So I told Chris Tescher that I was going to apply for a permit to build a house on the Pebble Beach side, which I did. It was on the side of Pescadero Canyon and looked down over a redwood grove and a creek, but it didn't really have any views. (In retrospect, it would have been great to build that parcel out. It would have been a beautiful house.) So, we went ahead and got the permit to build on the Pebble Beach lot, thanks to an old-time supervisor, Sam Karas, who got us the permit.

So there we were, we had the Pebble Beach side and were getting sued by the Friends of the Forest, Friends of the Trees, Save Pescadero Canyon group and the Sierra Club. We were also getting sued by Noel Mapsted and other like-minded "friends," who shared the notion that building was bad. It was all over the newspaper, all the time. "Developers Tescher and LeVett—another lawsuit!"

I went to the Del Monte Forest Foundation and I said, "Tell you what, there are about six acres there. I'll donate that building site, with the building permit and six acres to the Del Monte Forest Foundation. I want $300,000. We've got an appraisal of $800,000 for the whole property so you'll get a gift of $500,000 if you pay us $300,000.

And I said, there's one other catch. "We have gone through hell with this Pescadero Creek situation. He wants the Pescadero Creek dammed up so it would become the Noel Mapstead Harbor and the Noel Mapstead Lake. What we want, after all the negotiations, is for you to make sure that we get good publicity out of this. Great publicity, because we've been through a whole lot of crap. And so, all you old birds on the Del Monte Forest Foundation, you octogenarians, you see to it that we get lots and lots and lots of kudos for doing this."

We got it all set up and then came the Friday morning

when, at 10:30am, we were supposed to sign everything to begin escrow. The Del Monte Forest Foundation had cashed in bonds to get the $300,000 that we had already agreed upon.

But I received a phone call from Tescher at eight o'clock that morning, two-and-a-half hours before the signing of the escrow was to take place. As it turned out, Tescher and I had been interviewed about the deal by this hippy reporter from *The Pine Cone* and the article had just come out. Now, the whole front page was taken up with this story that said what a bunch of idiots we were, how greedy we were, and how we were developers of the worst degree. We were threatening to turn Pescadero Canyon into a sub-division, the headlines claimed!

It was horrible, and complete with quotes from Noel Mapstead stating that by suing us, they had stopped our project in its tracks. And by litigating, they had us running with our tails between our legs, because we couldn't fight him. His message was to sue the developers and stop the development. Don't let any growth happen in Carmel, Carmel Valley, Monterey County—no growth was the message.

When I finished reading the piece, I called the title company and told them to kill the deal. The buyers had breached the agreement. The PR was just the opposite of what we had said we wanted. That got the old geezers yelling, and telling the paper that now, *they* were going to sue *me*. I got hold of them and yelled, "You sons of bitches. Why were we doing this? Have you read the newspapers? It's not *our* fault, it's *your* fault. You agreed that there would be favorable articles and we'd get great PR out of this."

Carmel city officials were livid with Noel Mapstead and livid with the *Pine Cone* because they wanted this project, which would have stopped the lawsuit on their side. Tescher and I were so mad that we said: "We'll show them! We'll get editorial control of the local news!" We went to Chip Brown, the brother of the editor and the real owner of the newspaper. We negotiated with them and bought the Carmel Pine Cone for $1.2 million. Now, we had it under contract and we had a great editor who was also the owner of the *Sun* out of Carmel Valley, a newspaper that he and his wife edited and published. They had really great credentials and were going to become the new *Pine Cone* editors. But then, a family tragedy intervened and this poor fellow got deathly ill and had to go down to Arizona. Which left Tescher as the editor, and me selling advertising.

I said, "Tesch, there's no way I'm going to do this. This is the dumbest thing we've ever done. We'll just get ourselves in deeper and deeper and deeper. What if you sell the advertising, and I'll be the publisher and the editor? I'll do the letters to the editor and so on."

Tesch said, "No, no, no."

So anyway, we were lamenting closing the paper and trying to figure out what to do, when one morning in my office at Vagabond's House Inn, Paul Miller walked in and said, "Hi Denny, we've met before. I'm Paul Miller and I used to be at CBS, or whatever, maybe it was NBC."

He said, "I understand you bought the *Pine Cone* and I don't know how really interested you are, but I'd be happy to take over the contract. I heard maybe you guys weren't all that excited about moving forward and I'd like to own it. Can we work something out?"

I said, "Well Paul, I think we can." I sat down with Paul and we had a long conversation about how the *Pine Cone* had been a left-wing newspaper. He had to promise me that he would be middle-of-the-road; leaning neither Democrat, nor Republican. That he would be fair to business and fair to both sides of the track. I told him I needed this in writing. Paul agreed, and we've been good friends ever since. Oh, and very important, another part of our deal with Paul was that all the hippy reporters had to be fired! And they were. So it was all worth it in the end, buying the *Pine Cone,* the way we did, or didn't.

Strategizing with the Planning Commission

I was standing in my living room looking out at what I consider to be a million dollar view. Or is that view worth two million, or three million? I mean it's a spectacular view! If Hawaii were a bit closer, you'd have a perfect view of Hawaii. It is an astronomical view of the ocean. And views are worth a lot in Pebble Beach.

I've always believed in being the best neighbor I can be. In fact, I grew up believing it. So did my family. That you want to be best friends with neighbors, no matter what. I guess maybe that's why you call it a *neighborhood*. Even if you had a couple of hoods in the neighborhood, you called it a neighborhood.

A case in point—I bought a piece of property on Viscaino Road in Pebble Beach in 2004, and designed a house for it. But the county said, "Oh I'm sorry, you can't build a house there because you already have two houses. You can't build another house."

I said, "All I want to do is build garages for my car collection and put living quarters on top of the garage."

But they said, "No, we're sorry, Mr. LeVett, you've already got two houses on the property."

I said, "Well, I have to tear them down. Even though they're Comstock houses (historic fairy-tale cottages designed by Hugh Comstock) built in 1915 or 1918, I guess I'll have to tear them down."

They replied, "What? What? You'd tear the historic Comstocks down?"

I said, "Yeah, you haven't got 'em designated as historic so I'm going to go ahead and tear 'em down so I can build garages with living quarters on top of the garages."

"Um, er, well, Mr. LeVett, let's think about that. Let's

reconsider it a little bit."

My strategy worked and the county backed off, as they should have. Anyway, Anthony Davi, a dear friend and a Wild Turkey—that's the name of my lodge that I lived across the street from where I was building a house. If I built my house facing east, which I was planning to do, the width of the house would have blocked Anthony's view, his only ocean view. So instead I turned the house blueprint around so that it was angled East-West and provided a view corridor for him. Maybe it hurt the value of my house a little bit, because the house would have been better with a circular driveway with the front facing east, but instead, the front now faces the Comstock cottages on the property, and I was fine with it. I did it so Anthony would have a view. And jeezus, I felt good about that.

Of course, Anthony very much appreciated it. You do that for neighbors. You realize how important a view is, and especially when views are worth what they're worth here in Pebble Beach!

So I built the house. It took three years to build it. There were some complications that made it take a little longer to build. I want to say we finally moved in to the house in September of 2011. Now we hadn't even been there a year yet, and all of a sudden, I'm noticing trees in my neighbor's yard that weren't there before, and that were beginning to block my view. And I'm wondering, what the holy moly is going on?

So I called my neighbor, Steven Ames, and after he finally returned my three months of repeated phone calls, I said, "Excuse me, your trees are beginning to block my view."

He snapped back that my house had destroyed his privacy. "You absolutely totally destroyed my privacy. Therefore, I'm growing these trees to get my privacy back."

"Wait a minute," I told him, "I don't think you can do that because you're blocking a very, very valuable view."

He insisted, "You destroyed my privacy!"

I retorted, "The back of your house looks on the Comstock cottages and there's all sorts of trees between the Comstocks and your property. The only privacy that you're talking about is your driveway. And frankly, I don't care whether you're coming or going. I don't particularly want to watch you coming up and down your driveway, but you are ruining *my* view."

Well, in so many words, he told me to stick it in my, um, ear. I discovered that there's a Pebble Beach ordinance and a State of California ordinance, as well, that says you can't build a "spite fence." A *spite fence* is considered either a fence or trees that block a view, and that are planted purposely to block that view. I explained this to Ames, and he said it didn't make one bit of difference. "Go ahead, sue me!" he said, and so I did.

I couldn't, in my wildest dreams, see myself doing this to a neighbor; to plant huge trees on purpose to block their view. And just think of what it cost him to plant them! Like swamp pines, he had planted advance growing trees, meaning that they shoot up quickly, which was, of course, his intention. Because I so value a good neighbor policy, I wasn't just angry, I was sick about someone behaving this way.

Crash Resistant

While I called myself successful by the time I was 42, I certainly wasn't ready to retire. I mean, what in the hell would I have done with myself if I had retired? Anyway, "successful" wasn't that well off frankly, and yes, it was all real estate. Exactly the same thing I've done since 1961 — buy little apartment buildings, fix 'em up, and maintain them.

Everything was going pretty well until a few years prior. Did the crash of '08 hurt me as badly as others? It hurt everybody, but no, I didn't think I got hurt as badly as others. I know people who lost their businesses and their homes. I was protected because I could somewhat see it coming. The housing market especially. It couldn't keep going like that. It just couldn't. And as we all know, it didn't.

The big mortgage companies were writing loans to people who couldn't afford to rent a trailer. This was absolutely factual. Mortgage companies should not legally lend money like that but that's just what they did. In many cases, it was zero deposit down. I saw that happen back in the late '60s and early '70s, with the Savings and Loan banks. They would go by the appraisal, and everybody would be happy with a big appraisal, especially on property in good areas like Palo Alto. Of course, the borrowers had to be substantial, and happily, I was in a position to get a 100% loan. The only thing that bothered me was that these deals sometimes required fibbing. If you wanted a 100% loan, you had to tell the lender that the purchase price was higher than it was.

Of course, during the last 10 or 15 years, the lying was a massive problem. They were writing loans for people who didn't have the money to pay the mortgage, and never would. It wasn't just people with money. These people had nothing. If you couldn't see it coming, you were blind, because people who were barely hanging onto their jobs, who just had enough to get by, were getting approved for big loans. There was a news story about a field worker who made $14,000 a year and was approved for a $700,000 house.

You couldn't lend people like that money. It was inevitable that the market just had to crash. I had no clue it was going to be at the scale that it was. No clue it was going to end up in a worldwide recession; a virtual depression here in the United States.

I usually have a pretty good gut feel for the economy, but I haven't felt great about how we have been coming out of this; what they're calling The Great Recession. Yes, I know people are buying again and housing prices are shooting up and people with money are spending, but there are a whole lot of people who haven't seen anything they would call a recovery.

We're waiting for the momentum to really swing back up, but it hasn't. Matter of fact, I think that it's gotten to a more critical point, it's gotten worse. There are so many huge question marks and potholes in the road to a good economy out there. We've been in recessions before, but I think a lot of people expected us to be out of this by now. There's this desire to buy. To improve. But so many people are just making ends meet. They took jobs that didn't pay as well, and they're just scraping by, waiting for the good times to come back.

Okay, I see that economists say that the economy is doing better, even a lot better, but it hasn't reached the people on Main Street. Yes, the manufacturers are producing, but they haven't hired back the workers. A lot of people who thought they would lower their standard of living for a while, they're finding that they're stuck, and maybe lucky to have what they have . . . and then, Covid-19 struck . . .

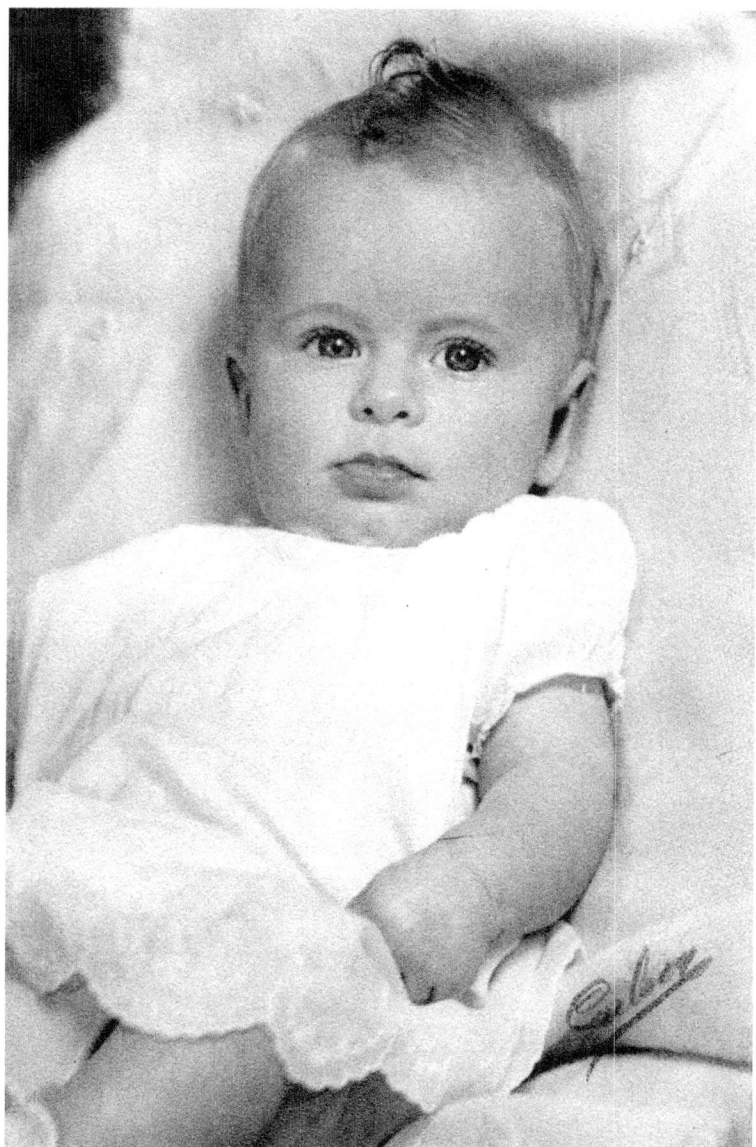

Dennis Albert LeVett at 5 months old

The little Cadet, approximately 3 years old

Mother Eloise, Denny, and his father Frank (1940)

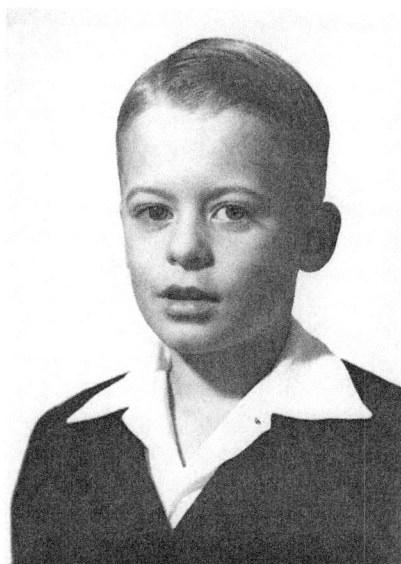
Denny (circa 1950)

Eloise Mayburn LeVett (1931)

Denny (left) with father Frank, brother Billy, and mom Eloise

Billy, Eloise, and Denny (1950)

Beloved Grandfather "A.J." (short for Albert Jonathan), also known by the nickname "Strutz" (his last name), was a tremendous influence on Denny's life.

Maternal Grandparents A.J. and Marie

Gun collector, Age 11

Pheasant season (1957)

College of the Pacific "Yell Leaders" (Denny second from right)

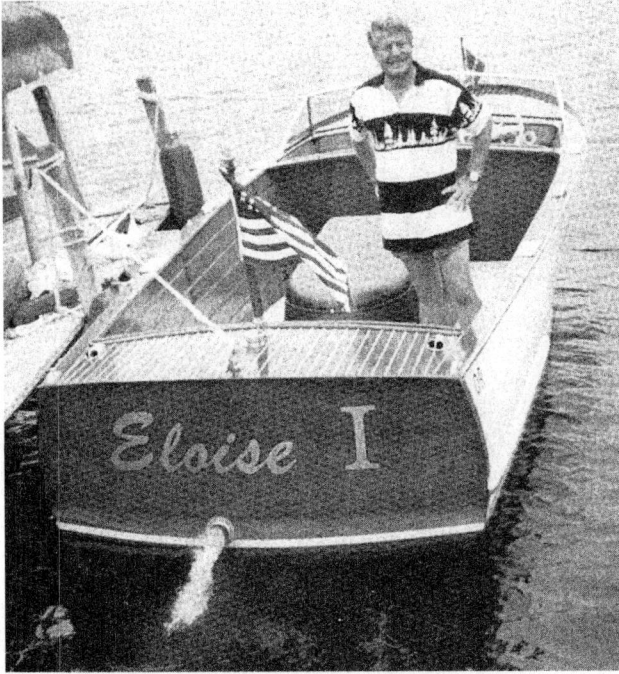

The "Eloise I" 1963 Chris Craft

Denny with an early Cessna 172

Fishing on Lake Okoboji

The Benbow Inn in Garberville, Humboldt County, California

Strutz I and Hyden I

Family photo of Denny and wife Karen with Kate and Amanda
(foreground) and step-daughters Amy (left) and Barbara (right)

Hyden I takes the wheel of a 1976 Ferrari 308 GTB

Partners of The Cypress Inn for over 34 years, Denny remarks, "I grew up in Iowa as a farm boy and my dream was to someday find a girl just like Doris Day. I'd never have guessed that one day I'd be in business with her."*

The Dealmakers: Denny with Doris Day and her son Terry Melcher (right). "Terry's Lounge" at The Cypress Inn is named in honor of Terry.*

*All likenesses of Doris Day courtesy of the Doris Day Estate

The dog-friendly Cypress Inn in Carmel-by-the Sea, California

THE PILOT

Through the Eye of a Tornado

Flying is something very different and very special, but even so, I hate flying in bad weather. I'm not instrument rated (meaning certified to fly under Instrument Flight Rules "in weather" or at night), although I have had the training and because I've had so much hood time. Pilots fly under either (VFR) Visual Flight Rules or (IFR) Instrument Flight Rules. I've just never taken the time to go get my instrument rating. Oh my god! Instruments!

Let me tell you about a flight from Red Cloud Airport in Minnesota to Chimney Rock, Nebraska. This was in a 1964 Cessna 182. I was flying with my friends Jerry Dunn and Jim Crowley. We took off from Red Cloud flying straight out over South Dakota through Wyoming and then down to Nevada, our final destination to be California. We had been out partying 'til the wee hours of the morning the night before, so when we took off, the other guys voted me as pilot because I wasn't hung over quite as badly as they were. We all hopped on the airplane and since I was kind of a music freak, I turned the radio on. I loved good music.

Heading toward Watertown, South Dakota, one of my points of navigation, little did I realize that there were horrendous crosswinds coming down from the North. I didn't have my license yet, but I understood navigation, of course, and I knew how to work the oars to steer the plane. So, I was just flying along nursing my hangover, drinking a little water and listening to the music, when all of a sudden I said to myself, "Wait a minute. I should have been over Watertown a half-hour ago or more. What the hell is going on? Where the hell am I?" So, I got my VORs going (VHF Omnidirectional Range equipment) and took a cross-check using Fremont, Nebraska as my point of reference. Jerry was a little more advanced than I was. He'd brought along a Jeppesen E-6 flight computer; the E-6 is more like a slide rule than a computer.

Suddenly, I was getting crosswinds and they were sweeping us like mad. I got my latitude and longitude configured, and then said, "Chimney Rock, Nebraska?! I'm supposed to be in South Dakota. What am I doing in Chimney Rock, Nebraska? For Christ sakes! Chimney Rock? Oh, shit!" (I'd invested in an oil well there that had gone bust, but that wasn't the reason for the expletive.)

It began to get really turbulent. So, I called ahead to Chimney Rock and requested a landing, "Chimney Rock Airport, 7-8-Sierra . . . I'd like to land at Chimney Rock."

The response was, "Sir, we're just closing the airport down. We have a really terrible sandstorm, and winds are gusting up to 50 knots."

I looked below us and could see the sandstorm over Chimney Rock. "What's the next airport? the closest I can get to?" I asked.

He replied, "Douglas, Wyoming."

Did I have enough fuel for Douglas, I wondered. I figured that even though I had a headwind (which causes the airplane to use more fuel when you fly against it), I had enough fuel to make it to Douglas. At least, I hoped and prayed that I did. I got on the Jeppesen computer trying to figure it out and according to my calculations, I better have enough fuel for Douglas, or if I don't, I should turn around right now. Which is really what I should have done.

I woke Jerry, who was asleep next to me. He had been flying 50 years or more. "Jerry," I said, "we've got a problem. I don't like this weather. I've got terrible turbulence, and we're all over the sky. I'm thinking about turning around and going back. We can't land at Chimney Rock, but we passed North Platte a while ago, and with the headwind we've got now, we could be at North Platte in no time."

"LeVett! You've got plenty of fuel to make it, what's the

next one? Riverton, Wyoming?"

"No," I said. "Douglas is going to be our closest choice."

"You've got plenty of fuel to make Douglas."

"I don't know if we do or not. Jerry. We've got 50-knot headwinds. I think this is cutting it too close, and the stupidest thing in the world is if we run out of fuel. I think we should turn around and go back. We're in terrible turbulence. That air up there scares the hell out of me. I have never seen more grizzly looking, protozoic-type squiggles of air in my entire life."

"Denny," he said, "You'll never be a pilot."

The visibility was terrible. All I had were clouds, big build-ups all over the place. Ahead of me was oily-looking air. Watertown Radio was broadcasting tornado warnings, so I purposely scratched Watertown from our original flight plan because it was too dangerous. Besides that, we had a hell of a northern crosswind. That 45-degree crosswind was why I was off course.

I said, "Jerry, I don't like this. I don't like the air up ahead. We've got to turn around."

Once again, he yelled "You'll never be a pilot! If you can see through it, you can fly through it, for God's sakes!" Well, there we were at 10,500 feet and it was getting more and more turbulent. The plane was bouncing all over the sky. At one point, it took two of us to hold the plane steady. And then, all of a sudden, it was smooth air and the plane dropped 5,000 feet without stopping. Can you imagine what that felt like? It went straight down. Not nose first, the whole plane!

All three of us had our heads banging on the ceiling of the cockpit. We all smoked in those days, so there were cigarette ashes and cigarette butts scattered all over the airplane, plus papers and miscellany on top of the fuselage as we plummeted downward. I didn't have any options. I had to maintain power, but I didn't dare do anything else because it'd rip the wings off.

Finally, I decided, "Forget it!" I pulled the throttle. I

didn't know what else to do. We continued to fall until we hit stable air at about 5,500 feet. I swear to God! I thought, "Here you go, Strutz!" I saw the wings go "whoo, whoo, whoo" like they were flapping. It was as if we were hitting bottom! Our bodies were smashed to the ceiling of the fuselage. And we're all just, at that point, scared to death. I mean I thought we were going to die. We were flying through an area that was probably 3,000 feet altitude. We could have crashed right into the ground without stopping.

I later learned that we had been in the eye of a tornado. It seems that we went through the trigger part of the tornado, and so it was a vacuum at the center. There was no air, which caused us to go straight down. At this point, I tell ya, I decided that I would never fly again.

As we approached Douglas, Wyoming, Jerry asked, "Do you think you can land it?"

"Right now, I don't have a tornado to deal with. It's clear as a bell. I have headwinds. We've got a straight approach to Douglas—I'll take it!"

So, now we're advancing towards a landing strip that is up on a plateau. I was flying in, getting my speed set to slow the airplane down and facing a cliff that was below us. Then, all of a sudden the plane sank again! The landing strip was above us and I was looking at the side of a cliff!

"Not again!" I fire-walled it (pushed the throttles to their forward limit) and trimmed back to stabilize. Whoooooo, I brought it up level with the plateau, all the while thinking that, for sure, this is the last time I'm ever going to fly again. Well, it was tough, but I did manage to get us safe on the ground. Whew! It was about eleven o'clock in the morning when we landed, and exhausted, we checked into a motel and went right to sleep.

Awakening about 7pm that evening, we all agreed to fly to Ogden—and that turned out to be the most beautiful flight in my entire life! When we took off, there was not a burble in the air. It was so peaceful. Of course, it was summertime, so it was still bright until about 9:30pm. When we got to Ogden, none of us wanted to go any further. We had a bite and went to bed.

I'll never forget that trip as long as I live. Going through the eye of a tornado. Not knowing what hit us. Thinking, as we were going straight down, "Well, this is it. I'm going to die." I don't have any sense of how long it took to drop 5,000 feet. No sense at all, because all we were doing was holding on. In those days we didn't use shoulder harnesses, so I just had a seatbelt on. My head was on the ceiling of the cockpit. I had the controls down in my lap. It was all I could do to hang on. Then just a few hours later, what a turnaround! The Ogden flight was so peaceful and beautiful that it gave me back my love of flying; that feeling of invincibility that only a pilot gets. I wanted to fly again.

Flying to the Super Bowl

This is the story of "The Flight of Twenty-Nine Palms." First, how the flight started. . . We were flying a Cessna 210 to the 1970 Super Bowl game at Tulane University Stadium. Fran Tarkington and the Minnesota Vikings were playing Len Dawson and the Kansas City Chiefs and there was no chance that Kansas City could beat the Minnesota Vikings. My friend Jerry and I were winging our way to New Orleans, and I was giving a ride to a couple of other guys who were going to fly commercial back. We were planning to meet two Swedish airline stewardesses and they would come back with us.

The plan was to cross Texas, with a stop in Houston, to drop someone off. The weather was lousy, but the reports we were getting from air traffic control and local towers were constant: 3500-foot ceilings and three miles visibility, which should be fine, but I never really felt the ceiling was ever that high. And three miles visibility? No, I never could see that far. In reality, I was flying along at 2900 feet, just under the clouds with *maybe* a mile visibility. It was horrible weather. Horrible.

We crossed over College Station and I contacted Houston, which was about 80 miles away. Houston has big problems with people flying at low altitude. The Jeppesen map, a reliable en route chart, shows radio towers all over the place. Flying under the clouds, you had to somehow wind your way around those towers. So, when I asked Houston for the weather, they said it was 3500 feet and three miles visibility. I said that sounds familiar. I told them we were just now over College Station and I was down to about 2400 feet. I asked if they could vector us in (guide us in by radio) because I was a little worried about the high towers.

They were vectoring us in; 4-3-Bravo this and 4-3-Bravo that, and so on and so on, and turn right. We were close to Houston, but just before we got there, I noticed we were icing up. I had virtually no visibility on the windshield. Jerry had been flying for a helluva long time, but he didn't have an instrument rating, which would have allowed us to navigate by the instruments, instead of by sight, and neither did I. I don't know what it was about us California boys not having instrument ratings. And another guy with us, Hank Wilson, who had wrecked my Cessna 175, was also with us. He didn't have an instrument rating either.

So there we were approaching the landing strip. I was following all the instructions that the Tower gave me. I was trying to stay straight and level. I informed them we had iced up, had no visibility, and were down to around 1800 feet.

I noticed the cylinder head temperature was in the red, which was dangerous because this could be an indication of a possible engine fail. The vents must have filled up with ice and snow. There was supposed to be automatic heating to keep the vents clear so the air would come through and keep the cylinders from overheating, but they were frozen shut. So there we were, with the engine sounding very rough. And the Tower was bringing us in. I told Jerry that I was thinking of declaring an emergency. But Jerry said you don't declare emergency. "You'll never be a pilot! Only asinine wimps declare emergencies."

I said, "Okay thank you Jerry, thank you so much for understanding." I shook my head as if to clear it and keyed the radio. "Uh, Houston Tower, 4-3-Bravo is declaring emergency. We have no visibility, we're iced over, cylinder head temperature is in the red. Help!"

They vectored us in and kept me on the glide slope, a radio transmitter that guides the aircraft to the center of the runway. While I didn't have my instrument rating, I did have some knowledge of flying by IMC (Instrument Meteorological Conditions). I got my cross VORs, got the needle centered steady, and then soon we were down low enough, about 500 feet and the ice was sliding off the wings and windshield. It still wasn't until we were at 200 feet that I could actually see. I put the plane down, taxied up to the flight service station, got out, walked into the place and said, "Excuse me. What do you have for visibility ceilings right now?" (the range of view lateral and vertical)

The guy told me, "We have 3500 feet, three miles."

That made me so darned mad! Jerry and Hank came in with me. And I said, "Guys, did you see anything that looked like, or in any way that resembled, 3500 feet and 3 miles visibility?" Their heads shook definitively "No!"

I told the guy, "At 1800, below the clouds we iced up. I kept calling you and you kept giving me 3500 feet, three miles. It wasn't 3500 feet and three miles!" God, was I mad!

The next morning we were at the airport at ten o'clock. The clouds were low; we were fogged in. And I asked the flight station guy, "How long is this thing going to last?"

"Oh," he said, "it won't last any time at all."

"What are you showing right now?"

"We're showing 3500 feet and three miles."

I said, "We know that's a joke, don't we."

He said, "You've got clearance to take off. You'll be all right."

We got in the airplane. Jerry was flying this time. We took off and at 600 feet we were in the stuff. Jerry said he couldn't fly through this. We radioed emergency. We turned around and came back. Now I can sound and look meaner than I really am. We landed, pulled up in front of the flight service station and I said, "Hi! It's only me again. What are you showing now for weather? Let me guess! 3500 feet, three miles, right? All right you guys, come out here with me." I was yelling at this point. "Come out here with me and take a look. That's what I call 600 feet and you call that 3500 feet? That's 600 feet! You go out and you fly through it. How many guys are you going to kill along the way? I heard 3500 feet, three miles all day yesterday coming from San Angelo and almost crashed with iced up windshield and iced up wings."

And one guy said, "Oh, I think I remember you. Oh my God!"

Finally, an hour or so later, we were still hanging out at the flight service station which is right there on the runway. I was asking, "Okay guys, what are we showing now?"

"We won't tell you."

It got to be a bit of a joke. We were actually laughing about it after awhile. Finally the skies cleared enough for us to get down to New Orleans, see the girls, watch the Super Bowl game and generally have a great time. The Chiefs beat the Vikings 23-to-7. Len Dawson, the Kansas City quarterback, was great; got the MVP. So much for what the experts were predicting. Instead of staying in New Orleans to celebrate, since Jerry had to be back in Palo Alto, we took off right after the game was over.

We got the girls in the back and started flying. And I said, "Okay Jerry, what we're going to do is we're going to fly to Phoenix and then home. With a 210 we thought we could make it from Phoenix to Palo Alto without refueling. The weather looked good according to the reports. So we took off and soon discovered that the best laid plans, et cetera.

Now this is January, and it gets dark early. And we've got mountains ahead of us. By 4:30, we were losing light. Again, the weather was coming down and down and down. I was saying, "I'm not going through this again. The weather is really coming in low. And we're flying to Palo Alto nighttime? I don't like flying nighttime anyway."

We had gotten a late start from New Orleans, and heading west, yes, we had winds. Plus, we'd already flown for a long time and we were all tired. At this point, I was flying and I said that we were going to stay overnight in Palm Springs. I called up Palm Springs Tower: "This is 4-3-Bravo, wanting to land Palm Springs." There was a lot of static coming back, and then we heard, "4-3-Bravo, Palm

Springs is fogged in. We've closed the airport."

I said, "Since when in January is Palm Springs fogged in zero-zero."

"Not very often," the Tower replied.

I said, "Okay, how am I doing from here to Bakersfield, to the Tehachapis? What's it look like?"

"You're going to have some low clouds, a little turbulence, a little headwind. I think that's the only choice now, unless you want to go back to Barstow."

I told them that we were forging ahead. Now it was dark. I mean, I couldn't believe what Palm Springs had told us, but they were right. It was solid fog — in January, when they always had the best weather! Now I was heading toward 29 Palms and getting lower and lower because the ceiling was coming down further and further.

I had flown this route many times, but I couldn't see a darn thing. I was counting on my VORs, which were tuned to 29 Palms and Lancaster, trying to pick my way through the Valley of 29 Palms. I knew I had mountains now on both sides. Lancaster was off there somewhere; Lancaster Air Force Base. I couldn't see a thing in front of me, and the light headwind had the plane all over the sky.

It was like being in a tornado. Jerry Dunn and I both were on the controls. I could basically only see wingtip to wingtip, nose to tail. The girls were in the back seat. Not just girls, but airline stewardesses on trans-European airlines. They were familiar with flying in all kinds of weather.

I couldn't see a thing except the lights on my panel. Even the map lights were bouncing all over the place. I couldn't dial in the VORs. I was trying to raise somebody on the radio — 29 Palms, Lancaster. I couldn't raise anyone, not even on 121.5, the emergency channel. I have to say, I was seriously afraid. This was worse than what I'd experienced in Chimney Rock, Nebraska. Nothing compared to this fear.

In my gut, right below my heart, it was the fear of death. In my brain, it was the thought that any moment now I could crash into a mountain. You don't know that feeling until you've been there. I even put my landing lights on at one point to see if I could see anything. I couldn't, but I knew we were below the tops of the mountains. Why didn't I climb? Icing, for one thing. Plus, the fact that any moment I thought we were going to be saved. Maybe something was going to save us.

Meanwhile, Jerry and I were yelling at each other. He was telling me, "Hey, this is no big deal. God! You'll never be a pilot!"

Boy, did I pray. I made promises to God that I'd never smoke, never drink, never have sex. Never tell a lie. The girls in the back were worried. They were screaming a little bit. They were seasoned stewardess but had never been in a situation like this. Few people had, who got out alive.

The situation was bad and getting worse. Then, I don't know how in the hell it happened, but all of a sudden I saw a bit of a shadow of the cliffs and mountains. They were a little ways away, but there was some sort of light in the sky and I was able to get the silhouette of the mountains. I didn't tell Jerry, I didn't tell the girls, because I didn't know what to tell them. Are we done for? Could we have flown into a box canyon and didn't know it? All the times that I had flown this route, I'd never flown this low into the Tehachapis.

I kept trying to get VORs to work; trying my best to get an idea of where we were. And all of a sudden it got really dark, and I was thinking, "Oh shit. This is it!" At that moment, and maybe it was because I was praying like mad, suddenly lights went on right in front of me. And by golly, it wasn't just some town, but gadzucks, a runway! The lights went on. Here I was flying like a madman, just trying to hold the plane steady and the runway lights went on! I didn't believe it! I pulled back on power, and pulled the nose up to slow the airplane down. Because the lights were right in front of me! I wasn't going to spend anytime circling and confirming what runway it was. I couldn't raise anyone on UNICOM (Universal Communications) frequency. I was just going to get the plane down. I didn't try to figure out how high I was or what the elevation was. I said, "Look, I'm going to be doing this by the seat of my pants because I have no clue!"

There was nothing to do but land the plane straight in. All I could think of was keep the nose up to lose speed. I needed power to deal with a 45-degree crosswind. The wind was so bad, I was holding onto the yoke like my life depended on it . . . and it did—plus, I was ruddering in (steering with my feet). I set the airplane down sideways and we went bump, bump, bump, bump, screech, bump, bump, bump! I pulled up in front of this shack that had lights in front of it. Just then, the lights went off. I was in shock. God, it wasn't my time, was it? It wasn't my time to go. I got out of the plane I walked up to the shack while Jerry tied down the plane.

I opened the door. I said to the guy inside, "First off, I want to thank you from the bottom of my heart! You saved my life, and three other people on that plane. The runway lights went on just before I was ready to hit a mountain and I landed here. So, thank you, and by the way, where am I? What is this place?"

"Hi! Glad you made it," he said." You're at Roy Rogers Happy Apple Valley Ranch."

"Roy Rogers Happy Apple Valley Ranch?"

He nodded his head.

I said, "How in God's name did you turn the lights on just the moment I thought was the end of my life and the lives of my three passengers? What made this happen?"

"Well, we were expecting a flight—a charter flight from Ontario Airport with guests arriving for a stay at the ranch to play golf and party; a little corporation thing. We normally have pretty good weather here. We don't tonight. The pilot radioed in to say that I should turn the lights on, but around 10 or 15 minutes later I got a call that they cancelled, due to bad weather. Couldn't get in. So off go the lights."

I said, "I don't know you. But I love you. You may not

know me, but you're my best friend. Is there a place where we can stay overnight?" God!

"Right over there is the hotel. Roy Rogers Happy Apple Valley Ranch," he said, "I'll give you a ride over.

We checked in and headed for the bar. Now one martini is the most I can drink. Apparently, I had three and I was on my fourth. I don't remember going to bed, and the Swedish girl I was with was gorgeous! And she probably drank a lot too. We didn't have dinner, we just drank. I was so happy to be alive! Next morning, believe it or not, the sun was out. We went in to have breakfast, all four of us at the breakfast table, and a guy walked over and said, "Excuse me. Are you the red and white Cessna 210 4-3-Bravo?"

And I said, "Yeah! Yeah! We are."

He said, "Sir, you didn't close your flight plan."

I said, "I want to tell you something. It was almost closed before I landed here. It was that hairy."

He said, "I know. We've got four planes that did not close their flight plan." He said, "I know for a fact that two of them are out there against a mountain and we were afraid that you were one of them. Congratulations! You made it!"

I said, "Sir, I'm going to tell you, I'm so sorry. This is the first time in my flying career that I failed to close my flight plan. I'm usually very conscientious about that. I was so grateful just to land. We almost crashed. I've never been so absolutely terrified in my life. I went straight to the bar. I didn't even think about the flight plan. I'm sorry. I must have put you through a lot of trouble."

He said, "You know, normally I would write you up. But under circumstances like this with several other planes missing, I'm so happy that you made it. It must have been one harrowing experience."

After this incident, I once again swore off flying. Well, that is, I didn't fly for about three months.

Flying into Mexico

What I used to do in the early Sixties when I was headed to Mexico was to fly from Palo Alto at 7:00-7:30 in the morning with a full tank of fuel. I started out flying my 1956 Cessna 182. What I loved about that 182 was that it was so perfectly rigged. It was the fastest 182 I've ever flown because the straight-back fuselage and straight-back tail had a certain aerodynamics to it. And I loved the design of that.

I didn't have autopilot; who wanted autopilot? As far as I was concerned, I loved trimming that thing up. But this 1956 182 was such a fine gem. I mean, if I had her today, that's the plane I'd be flying. I sold the plane to a real good friend of mine, Jim Biddle from Iowa Falls, who killed himself in that airplane. He was flying it back from Brownsville, Texas and well....

Why did I sell that plane? It was a hell of an airplane because I bought a 210—and that plane was fast! The '56 was a tail dragger with a nose wheel, (a landing wheel located under the nose of an aircraft). Cessna had moved the main gear back a little bit and put in a nose wheel. It was the old 180 tail-dragger with a single wheel at the rear of the plane to support the tail, and then, they moved it up front.

This was a 150 knot airplane. Flying alone I got 150 knots (one knot being equal to one nautical mile per hour). Fixed gear. The only other airplane that came close to it was that Hawk XP, which had the 200 horsepower engine. This one was 190 horse, but you could still boost it to produce about 210 horsepower.

I started flying a Piper Cherokee. And I never liked having to get up on the wing, open that one door, and crawl across. It always kinda bothered me because I constantly think about pilot safety. I mean, on a Cessna, there are two doors, two windows, and you were able to get in on the pilot side. I liked that it was easier than climbing up on the wings. Anyway, the '56 182 knew me, and I knew it. I knew the capabilities of that plane.

The normal route that I would take was to fly over the Tehachapis, go down Imperial Valley, and refuel at Imperial. Or I'd refuel at Mexicali. In those days, the price of fuel was so cheap in Mexicali. I just needed to be prepared to pay off every Mexican that I ran into. I had to pay $20 bucks — that was a lot of money in the '60s for a Ramsey Card. The Ramsey Card was needed to be able to operate your radio in Mexico. You always had to give them a Ramsey Card number. You also couldn't file a flight plan without one, and for every trip you had to pick up a new Ramsey Card.

I would fly through Mexicali because I hated going through Tijuana. Mexicali is right above Hermosillo and Guaymas. But Mexicali was port of entry. And boy, I tried to be nice to those guys. I always had plenty of cash to hand them because they would hold you up until you paid. They loved $10 bills. Those bills went a long way back then. So, fill up.! (Even Imperial gasoline was cheap in those days.)

You always had to check in at Imperial Airport on the return. You had to land and go through customs there. So you went through two customs, Mexicali at departure, and Imperial coming back. In the very beginning, this wasn't necessary. I'd file my papers, head to Mexico, and then, boom, over the fence. If I left at 7:00 in the morning from Palo Alto, with a stop in Mexicali for port of entry and fuel, I'd try to hold off and have lunch at Guaymas. We'd get in at 1:00 o'clock, after a six or seven-hour flight.

Then we'd have the best shrimp in the world. Huge Guaymas shrimp. Like eating a lobster! Unbelievable! The mariachis! The margaritas! This was at the old Union Pacific Hotel! It was Playa de Cortez on the Gulf of California, but on the mainland side of the Gulf.

We'd leave in the morning and try to get off by say, nine o'clock. San Blas was about a half hour out of Mazatlan.

You'd already be at altitude, but it was a half-hour even then. That was pushing it. I never made it to Puerto Vallarta in one stop out of Guaymas because I am talking six hours. I always figured I had a sure five hours out of the tanks. In fact, even in my own feeble mind I would think that if I conserved fuel and ran about 2200 RPMs that I could get 5½ hours out of it. But I never pushed it. I was so careful of never running short of fuel, except once when I was losing fuel out of the rocker arm and had headwinds coming back. More on that later.

Night of the Iguana

It was 1960, and I was on one of my first trips down to Mexico. It was my introduction to Mexico, really. There were four of us: Jerry Dunn, Denny Lucas, George Tondorf, and me. All four of us were pilots. The more experienced pilot was George Tondorf who flew 707s for Pan American. He was at the controls of a Cessna 182.

As you always did flying in Mexico, you listened to 129.9 Radio. That was the emergency channel and anyone in trouble would call that channel. (I think they changed it, or at least here in the States the frequency is 121.5, but in those days it was 129.9.)

We were flying along, and all of a sudden, we get an emergency call on 129.9 Radio. It was Thomas Olds from Albuquerque, New Mexico flying an Aero Commander. He'd just lost an engine. I think it was pretty heavily loaded and he was trying his best, but not having a lot of luck, to maintain altitude. We took cross VORs and located where we thought he should be, and believe it or not, we intercepted him.

At that point, we were maybe 80 miles northeast of Hermosillo. We followed him in to the airport, making sure that he made it. Watching him was really nerve-racking because he kept losing altitude. I swear to God, another 15 minutes and he'd have been down to five feet above the desert. But he made it in to Hermosillo and we followed him in. This was a port of entry, anyway. Thomas was so thankful. He said he could have gone down in that desert, but just knowing there was somebody there to follow him in if he went down was great. He thanked us over and over and then asked where we were headed. We told him our first stop was Guaymas, then down to Mazatlan.

He asked, "Why the hell do you want to go down to Mazatlan. Ugh!" I asked him where he was going, and he told us, "Puerto Vallarta, of course." He gave us his card and a brochure for the Tropicana Hotel in Puerto Vallarta, which he owned. He invited us to come down and stay for a week. "Forget about Mazatlan," he said, "only stay one night in Guaymas, and fly right down to Puerto Vallarta and be my guest, you guys, at Hotel Tropicana."

Oh Boy! Great! Love it! That would be my first time in Puerto Vallarta. Thomas told us that they're making a movie down there. It was *The Night of the Iguana* with Richard Burton and Ava Gardner. Our stay there turned out to be heaven! Absolute heaven! And there weren't too many Americans there. In fact, very few. I met a beautiful woman from Guadalajara, with a Castilian Spanish look. I had a great time with her and then I met another Mexican woman from Puerto Vallarta, and we had a ball, also.

At that time, there were two places to hang out, the Oceana Hotel and the El Dorado Hotel. That's where the greatest bars were. The El Dorado was right on the beach and everybody went there to drink. If there were a couple of gringos in town, that's where they hung out, with us at the El Dorado. I just loved it because I felt like I was a big time gringo. We spent an entire week there and I got to know Puerto Vallarta. I decided this was a place I wanted to come back to.

So when we got home, I made the decision to start buying property in Puerto Vallarta. At the time I was in partnership on a 182 aircraft and decided to buy my own—a beautiful 1956 182, red white and blue, with the tail number ending in 7-2-Bravo. During this period of time, I was making trips to Mexico every other month. Sometimes, every month. I'd fly down to Guaymas and then Vallarta. And then on the way back, I'd maybe spend a night at Alamos, maybe Hermosillo.

Of course, everybody welcomed an American who flew his own plane to Mexico. It was just wide open. All of a sudden, airplanes were flying in from all over. It just took off, so to speak, down there. Lots of private pilots flying in to enjoy Mexico. I started looking for property to buy thinking that this was going to be the future. I even considered starting a little airline in Mexico called Coast Central American Airlines from the California Coast down to Central America, which could be Guadalajara or Guatemala. Coast Central American Airlines sounded kinda cool. I had a card printed up: *President, Coast Central American Airlines*. I got a lot of mileage with that baby, let me tell you!

Oh, did I love flying to Mexico. It was a great experience. And though it took time to fly down there, there were a lot of other people who thought it was a good idea too. "Be nice to Denny. He might ask you to go along with him." Everybody loved it! Because they'd never seen Mexico like that. You know, you don't drive down very far with a car to Puerto Vallarta. It was too long a trip, the roads were terrible, and it wasn't really safe. Maybe you'd spend the night in Yuma, Arizona, and then drive down to Hermosillo or Guaymas. I loved Guaymas but not like Puerto Vallarta.

I was doing all the flying myself. Seldom was there ever someone else that could fly my airplane. Anyway, I would try to leave Palo Alto at seven in the morning and depending upon weather and winds, I'd have to stop in Calexico, then check out and tell the authorities I was leaving for Mexico. It was a waste of time, but that's what you did. Just over the canal or trench—a *river* they call it, but it was more like a swamp—we'd land in Mexicali.

Fuel was incredibly cheap in Mexico because it was government-owned. So my flight was usually to Calexico, then Mexicali for check-in and then Guaymas. Spend the night at Guaymas. In the 182 it took me six to seven hours to get to Guaymas. And then after Guaymas, it was roughly another seven hours to get down to Puerto Vallarta. And so it would be one fuel stop to get to Guaymas and then one fuel stop to get to Puerto Vallarta. We'd usually stop off in Mazatlan to refuel. Sometimes San Blas, but San Blas always had alligators and mosquitoes.

It was a long flight all along the coast. Right along the water and it was beautiful! And all those little villages! I used to swoop down on the villages to get a better look. Oh, I loved Puerto Vallarta!

It wasn't really Smuggling

When I went down to Mexico, it was hard for me to be gone longer than two weeks because I had a pretty thriving business in Palo Alto. So I would always try to make the trips meaningful in more ways than just one; the pleasure of the flight and the vacation-like atmosphere there.

I would try to buy hotels or beautiful parcels on the ocean; that sort of thing. One thing I knew for sure was that if you want to buy a place on the ocean in Mexico, you have to have a Mexican partner to be able to do it. So when I was in the process of purchasing the El Dorado Hotel in Puerto Vallarta, I took Salvador Escalante in as a 25% partner.

And in those days, if I wasn't buying property, I'd buy gold. A 50-peso piece was about an ounce and a quarter of gold. An ounce and a quarter of gold would cost $50. And the hard-sell price of gold was at something like $35 an ounce at that time. It was a pretty good deal and it was about par in buying a 50-peso piece for $50. So I was buying 20-peso pieces and 50-peso pieces, and bringing them back, though I never knew for sure if you could bring them back legally. Would they stop me at the border, and say I'm smuggling gold? I wasn't sure, so I always kept the gold hidden in my boots on the way back in to the States.

There probably was no problem at all bringing the pieces back, because, for goodness sake, they *were* currency. But it ended up that I had no problems carrying the gold back. No one even asked me if I had gold. I probably came back with maybe ten 20-peso or 50-peso pieces on every trip. They were, *and are,* absolutely beautiful, striking, gorgeous coins. (I still have most of them.)

You never really knew about what was legal in Mexico. One thing I did know was that you could not bring liquor back. Whether I would fly into the port of entry at Brownsville or Mexicali or Imperial, I'd stop at the border and the American customs agent would ask, did you bring any liquor back?

One of the best cognacs in the world was El Presidente cognac. It was so beyond good—oh, I wish I had a bottle of El Presidente cognac right now! You weren't supposed to bring it into the States, but I devised a scheme. If I was landing at Brownsville or Imperial for the border check, I'd have the bottles of Presidente well-hidden in the airplane. Then, when they would ask me if I had any alcohol, I'd say, "Yes, I've got a half a dozen bottles of tequila." The customs official would say, "I'm sorry. You have to surrender your tequila and pour it out."

It was a strange policy, it seemed to me, pouring the tequila out there on the tarmac. What a waste. But I would pour it out myself and mournfully say, "Well, it makes me very sad. Beautiful tequila going to the soil, or down the drain, et cetera." And that would take the pressure off bringing back the hidden El Presidente cognac (brandy), because then they wouldn't search the plane. I didn't do it every time—it would look kinda stupid, especially if it was the same customs official, but I did it enough times that I ended up with a pretty nice collection of bottles of El Presidente.

Going into Mexico, they always searched my plane, looking for guns. I wanted to take a gun with me for protection, in the event I had an emergency landing, but I didn't. You never wanted to land some place you hadn't planned on, which was a good reason not to fly at night. And a good reason to fly over villages and populated areas at all times. All in all, I made close to 50 trips to Mexico from Palo Alto. And that's a lot.

Flying to Mexico Again

I started flying down to Mexico again in the early '80s, some years after Echeverria was out of office. That would have been 1982. The higher-end Mexican tourist industry was trying to get American pilots back because we brought in a helluva lot of money. There was a good reason why we had stayed away.

Once I was coming back from Se Juan Teneo (also Zihuatanejo) with a couple who wanted to stop off and see Manzanillo. Manzanillo was where the Las Hadas Hotel was; where they made the movie "10" with Bo Derek and Dudley Moore.

Gordon F. was the guy who was with me on that trip and he was a jerk. We were coming into Manzanillo Airport and I was communicating with the Tower. They gave me the go-ahead to land, "Si, señor. You're clear to land on runway 3-1." But there was something wrong. It wasn't so much what I saw; I didn't notice anything amiss, but I sensed it. I was descending on final and still talking to them. "Okay. 7-8-Sierra. On final." But I didn't see anybody at the airport. What I did see were lines of airplanes on the ramp, next to the runway. There were all kinds of American airplanes— Cessnas, Bonanzas, Pipers, but there were no people around.

Of course, everybody in the pilot community in the States was talking about planes being confiscated in Mexico, but I'd never seen it happen. I knew, as every pilot does, that there is a universal rule that you never land on a runway with an "X" on it. It shows that the runway is closed, for whatever reason, maybe it's damaged, but you don't land on a runway marked with an "X." There was no "X" on the runway I was coming in on. No markings, no lights, no one driving a jeep waving flags. This was during the early '70s and the early days of the Echeverria administration, and with all the stories going around, I was really being careful. But Gordon was giving me a hard time, saying things like, "You don't have any guts. You're spineless." He virtually insisted that I land there. "Look at all the airplanes down there," he said. "And you talked to the Tower and you've got clearance."

I didn't listen to him. I remembered something about a new airport about 40 miles northwest of town. The new Manzanillo Airport, and this was the old Manzanillo Airport. It would be just like them to leave this airport open and every plane that landed got confiscated. "No," I said, "We're not landing, Gordon."

"Oh, you chicken shit," he spat back at me.

"Gordon," I told him in a voice that left little room for argument, "I'm captain in command. I run this airplane and you do what I say. We're not landing. Something is dastardly wrong." So we continued on to the new Manzanillo Airport and landed there without any trouble.

Afterwards, I went into the flight service station and told the manager that we almost landed at the other airport which was right in town. I mean, my God! The hotel we were going to, the wonderful Las Hadas Hotel, you could see from the runway. "Why," I asked them, "wouldn't we want to land there instead of a 40-mile taxi ride into town?"

I subsequently found out that there were so many villages and towns on the outskirts that the government was trying to increase tourist business from people passing through the new airport. There were some lovely beaches out there, and in fact, I stayed at a few hotels there in the '90s that were absolutely beautiful. They had been built because the new airport was located there. So that part did made sense. While speaking to the flight services attendant, he suddenly realized that I was the pilot who almost landed at the old airport. He said, "You were radioing and we heard you on the monitor."

I was getting hot. Why wouldn't they tell me to go to the

new Manzanillo Airport? Why wouldn't they tell me that I was landing at an airport that was closed and that my plane would be confiscated?

He replied in broken English, "Si, señor, that is very bad! We don't appreciate that because we lose tourism that way." He said everybody who landed there had their planes confiscated.

"But how was I supposed to know that it was closed down? There was no "X" on the runway and they cleared me to land."

"Señor, it doesn't matter. You land there and they take your airplane."

And that was what they did with all the airplanes. They were lined up as far as you could see. Then of course, the AOPA (Aircraft Owners and Pilots Association) Newsletter came out with "Don't go to Manzanillo! Don't go to the old airport. Mexico is not a safe place to fly anymore." Not a good place to fly during those days. That was for sure.

Looking for Sandy Riley

It wasn't just a crap-shoot; my picking Palo Alto as a place to start a business. Where else would you choose if you knew the Bay Area, were dating a girl from Palo Alto, and loved Palo Alto? Maybe I should say that Palo Alto picked me. Be that as it may, the real estate business was booming. In a good market or a bad market, you could always make a deal.

Of course, it was good when the market went down a little bit. The *San Jose Mercury News* would run a headline, "Property Values off 25% in Palo Alto." That was playing with numbers. As Mark Twain once said, "Facts are stubborn, but statistics are more pliable." And if you look back statistically, historically, the real estate market never dropped as much as five percent in Palo Alto. As I told a number of reporters from the *Merc*, if a house comes on the market at a time when the market has been hot, hot, hot, just pick a number, say $500,000 — it's like the owners are testing the waters. So maybe you put the house on the market for $500,000, but the house is only worth 400,000 and it sells for $400,000, does that mean that it loss 20 percent of its value? No. It was listed 25 percent higher than it should have been.

But the reporters never listened, or didn't understand. I'm not sure what they really understood, but inevitably they would report swings that weren't there. People always buy in Palo Alto. Palo Alto never had a 20 percent setback, much less a ten percent setback. Prices could be a little soft, but there certainly wasn't a ten percent loss. I'll never forget how *Time* and *Newsweek* depicted California houses falling off the cliff, as if there was a real estate collapse, especially in the Bay Area. So unfortunate.

I had met a very interesting, handsome hippy type who lived on his family inheritance. A heck of a great guy. I loved him. His name was Sandy Riley. And Sandy Riley's grandfather, the senior Riley, had invented the Riley Stoker. He was a railroad man, and if you ask me what the Riley Stoker was, I can only tell you that it was a device that stoked the engine on a locomotive. *I think.* Anyway, Riley had other railroad inventions under his belt because he was a railroad man. He invested in railroads and was quite successful. His grandson Sandy had a pretty good life. He had a 40-some-foot sloop and a half-dozen properties that he bought from me in Palo Alto. So, one day, he announced to me, "Denny, I want to sell all my properties. I'm going to move to Puerto Vallarta. I'm going to live in Central America. I'm going to sail for the rest of my life. So here is a list of my properties, which you know only too well. Sell them for me." So I did.

I had four offers in escrow, ready to go. I would contact him on his sloop by two-way radio. I got acceptances and had papers from the title company. I even had a power of attorney saying I was able to make deals for him. I bought three of the properties myself. Three of the properties I was very proud of because I had sold them to him originally and they were the gem of gems. I soon had escrows for all seven properties. He and I were to meet in the Mazatlan harbor on October 20th 1982. I want to say it was '82 because I stopped flying to Mexico after that particular trip, due to the fact that Mexican President Portillo maintained the policy of his predecessor, Echeverria—that is, to confiscate American owned airplanes.

I was waiting to hear from Sandy, but not getting any word. He was supposed to be in Cabo San Lucas on a certain date prior to our meeting. I called Cabo San Lucas Harbor, and they did not have Sandy Riley berthed there, so I assumed that he was keeping our date.

I decided to fly down in my 182 with Ron Nelson. Ron was the first graduate of San Jose School for Aeronautics, an instructor who was flying a U.S. Army Air Force C-141. Ron was the greatest guy in the world and we had become good friends. (I miss him terribly. He passed from a rare disease.)

Ron and I were flying south, heading for Hermasillo en route to Mazatlan. We found that we had high-altitude arcing, which is a mechanical problem involving the harness and the magneto (an electrical generator that uses magnets and coils) and which can result in losing fuel. Well, supposedly we got it fixed in Hermasillo as they taped up the harness. Yeah, they used Mexican tape, by the way.

Presumably, they had fixed it, but in the air on our way to Mazatlan, I said to Ron, "I'm checking the magnetos and it looks as if we still have high-altitude arcing. They didn't fix it."

Ron said we could try for Mazatlan Airport or Culiacan. "Mazatlan faces to the north," he said. "You'll find it about ten miles this side of downtown Mazatlan, right opposite that pointed piece of rock that's in the harbor. Or we've got Culiacan right here. It will take us from where we are right now, 15 minutes to make it to Culiacan."

I said, "Yeah, but Culiacan has drug and cartel problems. I don't want to land there. I really don't. We're kinda bouncing off empty (on the gauge), but we have enough fuel to make it to Mazatlan."

We kept going, banging off empty on both tanks, and I said, "Okay. There's Mazatlan straight ahead."

So, I radioed Mazatlan Airport, and said, "On final approach, declaring an emergency. We have high-altitude arcing of the harness and magnetos. We'll need a straight-in approach."

The Tower came back, "Señor, you are talking about the runway to the north of Mazatlan?"

"That's correct."

"That runway is abandoned. It is X'd out. We have the new airport 40 miles south of Mazatlan."

"Please give me an emergency landing okay, because it's getting dark. You can't fly a single engine at nighttime. It's getting dark and we are on empty. We have fuel leaking out of the airplane."

"Señor, you cannot. That is the rule. You cannot land or you will be put in jail." Whatever words he really used, I don't know, but that's what he meant.

Well, I wouldn't have given you a plug nickel for our chances of making the airport. I continued to plead with the Tower, trying to get through to a supervisor, "Señor, this is an emergency . . . an emergency!" But they wouldn't give us permission, and I didn't want to end up in jail. I said, "Okay. Not much of a choice, is there?" So we flew over downtown Mazatlan, nearby the Marina where Sandy Riley was supposed to be, and I was yelling out, "Sandy, don't worry. We're going to be a little late!"

The new airport was in sight and I hadn't lost the engine yet. I couldn't believe it. Of course, I was switching tanks back and forth and rocking the wings in order to get every drop into the engine. (How I loved having gravity gas tanks!)

I called the Tower for a straight-in emergency landing, using a base-leg approach for final. On the radio, I was saying, "Please, emergency." After diverting 50 miles with a leaking fuel tank, by the hand of God, we made a perfect landing at the proverbial *11th hour*, because the minute the nose gear settled in and the nose dropped down, the engine went off!

So, I said, "Okay, Tower. Okay, you guys. You see what happened? This a miracle! See, I wasn't kidding. We are out of fuel." Well, they pushed us off the runway and I had to get a new harness to fix the problem of the high-altitude arcing. It took them two weeks to do the job.

Meanwhile, that whole night and the next day at Mazatlan, we went in and out of the yacht club looking for Sandy Riley. There was no sign of him. We borrowed a plane and flew down to Puerto Vallarta to see if maybe he was there. But no Sandy Riley. So, we flew back to Palo Alto.

A month went by, and I was sitting with seven escrows and no Sandy Riley. I was calling every harbor, every marina, trying to find him. And then finally I received a phone call from him. Turns out he was holed up in one of his favorite old villages on the west coast of Mexico—and I don't mean on the west coast of the Sea of Cortez—this is the west coast of the Pacific Ocean in a village that he loved. He told me that he was coming up to Palo Alto, hopping a ride out of Cabo San Lucas in a Bonanza. So, I picked him up at the airport. He couldn't wait to sign all seven escrows and I had his check ready in just a couple of days. "Well, Congratulations, Sandy," I said to him. "Congratulations on getting your deal signed and getting your money."

It's funny how important some people can be in your life, and then they seem to disappear. I haven't talked to Sandy Riley now in over 35 years.

Landing Gear Down

I had a spiffy Skymaster that I learned to fly pretty well. Most people didn't like the Skymaster because it was noisy. But, in those days, it was the safest airplane in the air with an engine in front and an engine in the back. When you landed it, you had to virtually shut it off—not turn it off—but pull the rear engine all the way back to where it was just barely idling. That way, by keeping the engine on, it maintained the horizontal stabilizer way up and you were able to come in nose down, no matter what you did. You trimmed it like hell, and it didn't matter, because the engine in your rear was keeping that big horizontal double tail up. I really loved flying that airplane. Why? Because I could land it so well! I figured that even if I took off and lost an engine, I would still be able to fly that plane.

Then one day, I was coming into Palo Alto and I had another pilot with me who was going to fly the plane back to Monterey. As we were approaching the runway, I called my secretary to pick me up (the airport is only five minutes from my office). But as I tried to put the landing gear down, it wouldn't lower all the way. The main gear was only halfway down and the nose wheel was maybe about five inches down. That was it. I was sitting right over the side wheels, so I could see them because I had rear view mirrors up on the wings. I informed the Tower that we were doing a go-around, due to issues with the landing gear. Once again, I pulled the landing gear up to rotate it, and then, pushed it back down. And once again, the landing gear refused to go down all the way. The next time I started the rotation, I smelled that awful smell that you never want to smell—burning electrical wire. Oh my God! I had been in that situation before and it scared the little weenie out of me. So I called the Tower and said, "I'm gonna have to go around a couple of times and pump the landing gear, because I can't get it down." So around and around we went with my co-pilot trying to pump the landing gear down. I was flying. He was pumping. Continued flying. Continued pumping. Until, gradually, it went down just a bit.

I updated the Tower that progress was going really slowly and that we were not getting an awful lot of landing gear coming down. Just at that point, I received a phone call from my pal John Kerrz, and he said, "Hey, what's happening?"

I replied, "John I can't talk right now. I've got an emergency in the airplane. I can't get the landing gear down and they've called for an emergency landing. I'll talk to you later." Why I had my cell phone on I'll never know.

When John called my office for an update, they transferred him to my secretary, who was at the airport. She told him "All of a sudden, we've got ambulances, fire trucks, police, and a hook and ladder here."

Meanwhile, my co-pilot kept pumping while I kept in touch with the Tower. I flew right by and radioed, "How does it look from there?"

"Well, we can see that you haven't got the landing gear down yet, and the nose gear flap is not down either."

So I strategized, "Okay, if I can just get the nose gear flap down, and if I land real slow, it's going to force the landing gear out and it will lock in. Let's give it another couple of pumps." And in fact, a few more pumps and the nose gear clicked into place! So that gave me one leg. Obviously, the other two weren't down yet. But at least I had a nose gear.

I called the Tower again, and said, "We're gonna try it." Then, I came in really slow, full flaps, holding the Skymaster off the ground as long as I could. Trimmed back. Nose up. And with literally nothing on the rear engine, so I had that tail sinking down where I wanted it.

Coming in, I decided, "I'm gonna hold one foot off for as

long as I possibly can." Using the very beginning of the runway, I purposely slowed the plane down so that the stall warning horn sounded, and trimmed back. I used the throttle that way so I could feel it. And I absolutely *did* feel it. Sinking, sinking, sinking. It was the best landing I ever made in my life! I just touched the ground, and the landing gear went "boom" and locked! I said, "We made it, we're home free!" All these horns were honking and tooting. The big fire engine "woo woo'd." Everybody—I mean the whole place—was lined with ambulances, cop cars, fire engines and more fire engines, and the hook-and-ladder truck. It was a celebration. A wonderful celebration. I taxied the plane to my tie-down, and everybody met me there.

A call came in from my then-wife Karen. "What's going on?" she said. "What, what happened?"

"We had a little landing gear problem, but I made it."

"Well, they told me that the hook-and-ladder truck was there," she said. What was the hook and ladder truck doing there? Tell me! Why the hook and ladder truck?"

So my tall tale began . . . "It's okay, Karen. I couldn't get the plane down because I didn't have the landing gear. I was scared to death that the plane could blow up if I hit the runway or if I came in with no wheels. So the firemen brought in a hook-and-ladder truck to put the ladder up so that it was about four stories tall. That way, when I flew by, as slowly as I possibly could, I would open the door, grab the ladder, and climb down."

"Oh wow! Oh wow!" she exclaimed, "Oh, that's good, Denny. Okay, talk to you later!" Click.

She told the story to a couple of friends of hers. She relayed, "Denny grabbed the ladder of the hook-and-ladder truck and walked down the ladder from the airplane." Boing! Cuckoo, Cuckoo! People who knew Karen would just laugh! But that was Karen. Her mind was always all over the place. And "Oh wow! Wow, Denny! Oh, that's neat!" I told this story all over the place. You had to know Karen.

Finally, a Pilot's License

There's a sidebar to the flight with Ron Nelson. The year was 1966 and I had been flying for about three years without a pilot's license. I finally decided, well, insurance-wise and with owning my own aircraft, I thought I'd better think about getting one. So, I told Ron, who was a flight instructor at the Palo Alto Flight School, "I need to get my pilot's license."

"Well, how long you been flying, Denny?"

"Oh, I've been flying three years."

"And you haven't gotten a pilot's license yet? Let's go out and I will give you some training and I will get the pilot's license for you."

"We can take my airplane."

"What kinda airplane do you have?"

"I've got a 182."

"You're flying that and you don't have a pilot's license?"

"No. Never needed one, really. I fly to Mexico all the time. Nobody has ever asked me for my pilot's license."

So I took him up in the 182. We did power-on stalls and such things. I knew what I was doing, after all, I had hundreds of hours in that 182. He saw that I could fly. Ron said, "I'm taking you to Dee Thurman right now."

I knew Dee was an FAA flight examiner and, as it happened, she was free, so I took her up. And as we flew, I explained everything I was doing. We pulled off the ground quickly. I was climbing at such-and-such a rate. I was raising flaps, turning in a 45-degree bank. And of course, I was doing all my radio work. Here I was explaining absolutely everything I was doing.

We got up over Livermore, and I was at 5,500 feet. I told her, "Now we do a power-on stall." Nobody likes a power-on stall, especially when you've got somebody who doesn't have their pilot's license flying the aircraft. I explained what I was doing. "I'll pull the nose up until the air speed starts dropping off. Remember, the left wing will fall off and we'll start a spin, but I will rudder it out of the spin, rudder it back down and we'll pull out not losing more than 500 feet."

She said, "Mr. LeVett, take me back."

"Excuse me, Ms. Thurman?"

"Take me back. There's no getting around it. You know how to fly this airplane."

I came in for a perfect landing. And she said, "Come on. You've got your pilot's license. It certainly took a long time to get. And you certainly got an awful lot of flying hours in between, didn't you?"

Yes . . . indeed, I did.

GUNS, GUNS, AND MORE GUNS

Guns in My Youth

Matt Kickles owned a fascinating museum in Iowa Falls featuring one of the largest gun collections in America. Matt decided to sell his museum and was in the process of weeding out the stuff that nobody would want, and that left more things for me. Since they were leftovers, some were broken or just junk, but there was a pretty good gunsmith in Iowa Falls, so I was able to fix them up.

I'd go down every Sunday to see the guns at Matt's museum and every Sunday he'd give me another gun. I recall one day he gave me a '49 Colt pocket 19, and I said, "Matt, it doesn't work." What he probably wanted to say was, "Hey kid. You're lucky to have this." But instead he went into a back room and returned with a Colt '49 pocket, which I still have. It has raised carved ivory grips. It is beautiful! It is one of my prized possessions. They called it the Colt '49 pocket back then, because you could carry it in your pocket, but it was a serious gun, about 7 inches, with a 4-inch barrel. Matt also had a stock of automatic weapons, including a .50-caliber machine gun from the nose of a B-17 and a couple of .30-caliber machine guns. When as a youth, my father and grandfather wouldn't let me have them, it was probably the biggest disappointment of my early life. Oh, I wanted those machine guns; and to put one of them on the front of the tractor. It would also be good to shred pheasants, or for deer hunting. We did have a lot of deer back there too, including Mule tail and white tail deer. That was before I realized that I didn't want to shoot animals.

By the time I was ten or eleven, I had a pretty good size gun collection, including a British Sten gun and a German Schmeisser, both 9mm and both machine guns that were prized possessions of mine. In 1956, when I was in my late teens, I sold them to a dealer in Des Moines who took them to Miami, and then to Cuba. I did this a number of times with my contact. I'd make a phone call, tell them what I had; we'd negotiate a price and then he'd drive up for the guns. Most of the time he'd be getting a dozen or more guns. The guns were for Fidel Castro. He was the freedom fighter at the time, and back in the '50s, he was a handsome guy. We all wanted to be like Castro. So this was a kinda patriotic thing we were doing. America felt the same way. That we were doing the right thing to help get rid of the dictator, Fulgencio Batista, so that somebody would help restore the wheels of commerce in Cuba. What little we understood about Castro. How wrong we were! Oh my God!

I was selling guns all through the mid-fifties to the guy in Des Moines. Why Des Moines, you ask? Well, this was the center of Iowa. Iowa had lots of game, lots of forests, obviously lots of fields, and everybody could own a gun. You could buy anything. You didn't have to register guns then. You'd just say, "Hey, wait a minute. How much is your machine gun? $25? I'll give you $20." All right, you've got a deal.

I was running around to gun shows all over, buying up any M1 carbine or Garand semi-automatic I could find. I mean you could, no questions asked, sell a Springfield bolt-action 30-odd-6 caliber, which was popular, too. I was picking up every one of those I could possibly find. There was also a pretty good market for selling cheap Saturday night specials, though that's not what they called them back then. I'd buy them for $2 or $3 and sell 'em for $10 along with a few cartridges. That really made the sale.

In addition to the buying and selling of guns, I had my car and boat washing and waxing business, and my lawn business. I started my various businesses when I was 13. I would go from house to house and set up a kind of verbal contract with my customers to mow their yard. In Iowa, in the summertime with that rich soil, and the rain we'd get, I mean in two days your grass needed mowing. So it was a pretty thriving business in the summertime, let me tell you. I used a rotary mower. That was the best thing when rotary mowers came on the scene because they were quick and easy to use. When you pressed that lever to the forward position and it took off on you, it was like riding an Iowa hog. I did my share of damage with that one. But thanks to my grandfather, who bought me the mower, plus a push mower and trimmers, I had a regular edging, trimming, and mowing business. Most of my clients needed to have their property mowed twice a week, so I'd make a dollar to two dollars, which wasn't bad. I could do a yard in a half hour.

Depending upon how dirty the car was, a washing and waxing could cost $5 to $10. I'd call people up and say, "Mr. Schumacher, can I wash and wax your car and do your whitewalls, et cetera?" It was a grand little business. For boats, I did the same thing. I had a pretty good-size Boeing boat trailer with a hitch, so I'd pick them up and wash them.

I enjoyed a pretty enterprising childhood as I was growing up. I remember I used to get away with almost anything in Iowa Falls. Within reason, of course! They didn't have brothels in the middle of town. And they didn't like to have gangsters living there. In the '20s and '30s, a lot of 'em, gangsters, I'm talking about, did come to town because it was one of those places you could hole up easy. Like at the Woods Hotel.

As a young boy, I wasn't really aware of the external forces. We had a nice backyard with a flagstone barbeque built up pretty high. Everyone barbequed in those days. I would sit on my back porch and with my .22 rifle would shoot cans off the barbeque. I would also go running through Foster Woods behind our house. I pretended to be Daniel Boone, or Hawkeye, or James Fenimore Cooper ' characters from *The Deerslayer* and *The Last of the Mohicans*. I loved, playing Cowboys and Indians. Really and truly, it was the greatest place to live and grow up.

The Reluctant Hunter

In Iowa, we had grouse, woodchucks, quail, ducks, and geese. And there was just unbelievable pheasant hunting. I hunted pheasant. You'd never shoot one on the ground. You've got to give 'em a sporting chance. Of course they're horrific fliers, so some chance. They're fast and they're all over the place! That's part of the sport. I didn't like duck and quail hunting because I loved ducks and quail. I wasn't too hot about eating them either. Not when we had Iowa corn-fed beef around. So, just as I was reluctant to shoot a rabbit or a squirrel, I was reluctant to shoot a duck or quail.

My wife will seriously dislike that I'm saying this, but God created pheasants so that the men would have something to do on weekends and their wives could get rid of them. Men worked five days a week, and then on the weekends, they'd go hunting for deer, quail, and duck and pheasants, especially. I built a hunting lodge that sat over the valley where I was raised; on the Little Sioux River and forest. It is one of the most beautiful sites, loaded with pheasants until a few years ago.

In 2015, I talked to Bill Bowes on the farm next to mine in Milford, Iowa, and Bill said, "I go out for a 2 ½ mile walk everyday and I haven't seen a pheasant." There were only 200,000 pheasants in the whole state versus a normal 20 million. That's not a lot of pheasants.

I still hunt. I use a 12-gauge shotgun, and a 410, 20, 16 and 12. One at a time. They each have their purpose. I love my 16-gauge double. I don't shoot my 20-gauge very often. I love my 410; it's the same 410 I started shooting with when I was eight years old — double-barreled Crescent Arms. I clean them myself.

Colt Paterson

I was in my twenties before I bought my first Colt Paterson firearm. They were the top of the line—the most collectible and most sought after of all the pistols. I now have a significant collection of historic Colts; and actually, my collection is the largest in the world. This was documented by R. L. Wilson in a book entitled *The Paterson Colt Book: Featuring the Dennis A. LeVett Collection,* which was released in 2001.

I had a Colt rifle in my teens, but I bought my first Colt Paterson pistol at the 1961 San Jose Gun Show for $2100, and years later, sold it to a friend of mine, Gabe Nola, for $40,000.00. I always regretted that sale and finally bought it back from him for $70,000.00 in 2019.

My fascination with guns wasn't about emulating Wyatt Earp. I grew up in this wonderful wooded town with waterfalls and half a dozen different rivers that was a great place for hunting. When I was a little boy, I played cowboys and Indians and never missed a matinee at either the Metropolitan or Rex Theater on Saturday afternoons. I'd always go to the movies to see Johnny Mac Brown, the Durango Kid, or Red Rider. Saturday was sacred. You could even get in to see two matinees and two cowboy movies.

But to stress the point, I don't collect guns to defend my homestead. Of course, I would if need be, but I don't expect to have to. It really has a lot to do with rarity and value. Take for instance, the Colt Paterson, a gun that I could never afford to buy until I was in my 20s. They started making these guns in the early nineteenth century. It was the first revolving pistol, replacing the flintlock pistol, that in 1835 was known as the Collier Revolving.

Then, the 1830s saw the advent of the fulminary

mercury cap. This was a little brass cap that you would put on the chimney. Now you'd have the cylinder, and in the early Colts, five chambers with five chimneys. When the hammer hit the cap on the chimney, a spark would fly through the chimney to the chamber where there was black powder and ball. That was a great invention, probably one of the greatest inventions in "gun-dom" in the 1830s—the fulminary mercury cap and the percussion. Not flint, because they were all flint before that. The percussion rifle or revolver was the successor to the flint firing mechanism.

Now in 1836, about the only guns there were throughout the world, military and personal use, were either the single shot, flintlock musket or pistol, or flintlock double-barreled rifle or shotgun or pistol. There were all sorts of varieties. There were no bullets. They were all powder and percussion cap or flint.

Then in 1836, Sam Colt got the patent in the U.S. and England for a revolving pistol and a revolving rifle. The rifle, if you can imagine this, from a single shot flintlock to a revolving percussion, eight-shot revolving percussion rifle. It was simple. After you fired the eight shots you simply pulled the barrel off, replaced the empty cylinder with a full one, put the barrel back on, and you were ready to fire. It was revolutionary. You could almost equate it with the machine gun that Gatling developed three decades later. And there was also the five-shot pistol where there was only a single-shot handgun before.

It is ironic that the Colt revolving rifle and pistol came out in 1836, which was the year when the Battle of the Alamo was fought. Unfortunately for the defenders, they had none of the new guns. The Alamo guns were almost all flint, like the old Kentucky rifle. Davy Crockett and the others had to tap the powder down the barrel, drop the ball in on top of the powder. Ramrod it down.

By end of 1836, the government had ordered 100 revolving Colt Paterson rifles. The reason that the order mentioned "Paterson" was that they were made at the Colt factory in Paterson, New Jersey. The Paterson Waterfall, the second highest on the East Coast after Niagara Falls, turned all the paddle wheels that generated power for a number of manufacturers there. Paterson was actually a center of the Industrial Revolution in the 1830s and the 1840s.

The army ordered the 100 rifles to fight the Seminole War in Florida. The first 50 were sent down to Florida in a boat that was caught in a storm and stuck in sand. So the next boat went out with 50 more rifles on it. They made sure to get a couple of very calm days to sail down so they wouldn't lose those rifles. (There were only a total of 200 ever made, with probably only 20 of them left, and I've got three of them.)

Now, this you won't believe. The Army put together a squad of men, the (Colt) Paterson Revolving Rifle Squad, who practiced with their 50 Colt Paterson revolving rifles. Good idea. They had an encampment the first night in the Everglades and they stacked up the coveted Colt Paterson rifles, but those pesky Seminoles came in and stole 25 of them. Now we have an even playing field—twenty-five Colt revolving rifles for the Seminoles, and the 25 remaining for the U.S. Army.

True story. And, there are so *many* stories about the Colt Paterson. Like in 1837, the Texas Rangers got their hands on the first .36 caliber revolving 5-shot Colt Paterson, 7 ½ inch barrel or 9 inch barrel. Everybody carried two. That way they had ten shots, plus extra cylinders.

John Coffee "Jack" Hays was a famous Texas Ranger when his group, of about 18 men, were attacked by a horde of Comanches. The Comanches had a trick of sending a couple of Indians to run out against the Rangers to provoke the Rangers to fire at them. But after everybody fired, they all had to reload their guns, and that's when the Comanches would all attack. That didn't happen this time, because the Rangers all had revolvers to cut down the Comanches. That was one of the most famous guns ever, and even today, among the most coveted firearms in U.S. history are the Colt

Paterson rifle and pistol. Later on, Captain Walker of the U.S. Army, along with Sam Colt, produced the Walker revolver, which was a .44 caliber and considerably bigger. I mean, it was a horse pistol. When you fired it, you actually had to use two hands.

My interest in these guns is not about killing people. It is their role in our history. It has long been said that the Colt 1873 .45 six-shot revolver was "the gun that won the west." And a case can be made for that, but that gun came along almost four decades later. The beginning phase was in 1836-1837, way up until 1848, when the Baby Dragoon and the Dragoon, which were offshoots of the Colt Patersons and Walkers, came in. It's a hell of a history. And that history is what really got my attention.

Dealing with the ATF

Because I've bought and sold and traded many, many guns over a lot of years, I have had a lot of contact with ATF (that stood for the Bureau of Alcohol, Tobacco, and Firearms. Now they have added Explosives.) One day, I received a very unpleasant call from ATF. This was 1978, I think. I was in Palo Alto. They wanted me to help them put a sting on someone. There was a gun collector up in Gridley, California — a guy, we'll call him Roger — who was just a hell of a character. I had worked on his ranch and he and I were talking guns all the time. Roger had sold me a couple of his Thompson submachine guns. Hell, I had known about Thompsons because I had owned a few and was required to get special permits from the ATF.

The ATF told me they wanted to use me to set him up and arrest him. I said I didn't want anything to do with that. I knew Roger and I liked the guy, and I had worked for him. He had been good to me in this little town, Gridley, which was where my mother lived, as did my brother, who also worked for him.

They said, "Well, you have to help us."

I said, "I don't want to."

So I got a phone call from Roger and he told me that he had gotten a call from somebody who said he wanted to buy machine guns, and would I be interested in selling mine?

I told him, "No, I wouldn't be interested and I don't want to be involved. I've already had a phone call from an ATF operative."

He got it right away. "Oh, you're kidding? Really? So I'm being set up?"

I said, "Sure sounds like it to me."

The next thing I know, there was a bomb scare at the

local Dean Witter stock brokerage office. It didn't go off, but they found the bomb, and they detonated it. The ATF said they had a tip-off that I had planted the bomb. I told them that was absurd. "I'm a successful local businessman, why would I do that? What reason would I have to do something like that?"

Well of course, they didn't have any reason. Then a few weeks later, I was at the Mountain View gun show and a couple of ATF agents stole a couple of the Walther semi-automatics from my table. Then they said they wanted to borrow my car, which was an old Mercedes Benz, a '58 classic. Soon I heard stories that an old Mercedes, like mine, had been used as a getaway car. Of course, it was a phony story. Obviously, they were trying to frame me, because as it became clear to me later, you don't say "No" to the ATF. Especially when you bust up a sting they've set up.

Anyway, when they brought the car back to me, the clutch no longer worked. They stole my guns and brought back my car without a clutch. When they came into my office, it was very embarrassing. They said, "Mr. LeVett, we're going to have to take you in."

"No, you're not. For what?"

"On Monday, we'll need you to come down to the ATF Department at the Federal Building in San Jose."

I alerted my attorney, but when Monday came around, the ATF said, "Well, no, we're not going to take you in. We want you to take a lie detector test."

You can imagine what I was going through by now, with all the bad things I'd heard about these guys—people who worked for *my* government and were paid with *my* tax money. Horrible. So anyway, I went to Oakland to take a lie detector test. It was handled by a really neat guy who was the captain of detectives of the Oakland Police Department. He took me into his office for the test, leaving the ATF agents outside. Then, he said to me, "Look, these ATF guys are the absolute worst in the business. They go around trying to persecute people all the time. When you told them you wouldn't participate in their sting, that you wouldn't sell out a friend or get a friend involved, you were dead meat. They were going to get you."

I took the lie detector test and when I finished, the guy was upset. He said, "Jesus." He summoned the ATF agents into his office and called them scumbags. He said, "You guys don't ever, ever do this to me again. You shouldn't do this to anybody. You have taken his rights away and you were going to make him pay for the fact that he wouldn't go along with you. This guy passed the test as clean as a whistle. I'm going to file a complaint against you guys."

This was the Oakland PD Captain of Detectives telling the ATF what he thought of them. I sure felt vindicated. Anyway, I saw the AFT agents some years later at a gun show. At the time, they were persecuting someone else. And I said to them, "Never in my lifetime would I have ever believed that anybody that worked for the United States government could be as low life as you guys. If I had the time, I would do everything I could to get you guys kicked off the force." Oh, jeez, I was mad. I have never forgotten that.

And about my friend in Gridley, I don't think they ever got him, though I think his guns were confiscated. But at least he never went to jail.

Packin' Heat

It used to be that in the '50s and '60s you would buy things by paying with your own money because you were brought up right. You didn't go around threatening people or shooting at them.

I remember once driving my MG down the main street of Iowa Falls and laying alongside me in the car was an old 1866 Cowboy Winchester 30-30. The police chief stopped me and said, "Denny, Denny, Denny, you know better than that—you can't be riding with a rifle sitting in the front seat of an open car. You just can't do that. That's menacing. So I'm going to take possession of that rifle and bring it down to the office. Think it over for a while, then come by and pick it up tomorrow."

Boy, that made an impression on me. But wait a minute. If I've got a gun in my car and I have it put away under a blanket in the back seat, that's a concealed weapon. But if I'm riding with it in the front seat of my MG, it's not a concealed weapon—it's a menacing weapon. I didn't think that made a lot of sense. It should be about the person and whether he was safe to have a gun, rather than whether people could see I had a gun.

You think back to the days of the Wild West when people were riding through a cowboy town, Laramie for instance, and they would carry rifles and wear pistols in their belt, openly. Of course in this modern world it's frowned upon now. It's is a very interesting study of the transition and evolution of free people carrying guns.

I don't think it was until the last thirty or forty years that you ever heard of someone walking into a school and shooting people. Now we're almost not surprised when it happens. And that's with stricter gun laws. It doesn't seem to make much sense, at least not to me.

I will say this, for anybody who is truly in danger, it may make sense to carry a gun. But with today's laws, I don't know if you want to get a concealed weapons permit, because at least in California, people who have a permit are publicly listed. You can actually find out online who has a concealed weapons permit. That doesn't make sense to me.

I mean, if I felt I needed to protect myself, I would think twice about getting a permit. I think I would rather go before a jury on a weapons charge and defend myself. As one of my policeman friends said, "It's better to stand before a jury of twelve than to be carried off by six of your friends."

Packin' Heat (2)

There was a time in my life when I carried a gun for protection. It was circa 1965. I did so at the suggestion of the police chief in Palo Alto, a good fellow named Hydie. (That was his last name, of course, I don't remember his first name. I always called him "Chief.") This was when, not long after I came to Palo Alto, there were three or four of us business people who were on the assassination list of the Weathermen, the Enemies of Che Guervara, and one of the early alternative publications of the 1960's, based in College Terrace, on College Avenue in Palo Alto. I was on the list because I was regarded as a "Landlord Oppressor."

As I remember, it was a big deal being on an assassination list. Kinda like being on Nixon's *Enemies List* or Joseph McCarthy's infamous "list" of Communists, and here I was, on three of them. It was sort of funny, and sort of not. Mostly it had to do with my owning apartments. I owned a big apartment building up in College Terrace. It was on a large piece of land and I had something like eight units in the building.

I remember when Bob Columbine came to me and said, "Denny, we want that building and the cottages as our campus for what they called, the "free university" and press.

Bob Columbine used to be a friend of mine. I knew Bob when he was wearing regimental three-piece suits and ties. We used to hang out and drink beers together, and now he was the head of this university group and had gone very hippy.

I said, "Bob, what are you talking about, you want that house?"

"We're going to turn it into a university, a free university," he said. "We want you to donate it to us."

"And what do I get in return?" I asked.

"We'll be nice and take the pressure off your public image. We'll write good things about you in the press."

I said, "Bob, you really surprise me. I remember when you used to be a businessman. How could you think I'd just give it to you?"

"Well Denny, yeah, yeah. We could buy it from you, but you're gonna need to donate part of the cost."

"I'm going to donate part of it to the University Press? To the group that bashes every business owner in town? Bob, are you out of your mind?"

Then he wasn't nice anymore. "Okay then, Denny, you're going to pay for this. Wait and see, you'll pay for this."

So what they did was make a poster that showed me in front of this house I had on Tasso Street, this old Victorian. It showed me in a black hat and a mustache as I was evicting a woman and her baby. That was me, the Landlord-Oppressor LeVett. That's how I got on the first assassination list. Then came the other groups. There was the Weathermen, the Foes of Che Guevara, Friends of Che Guevara versus the Foes of Che Guevara. It was nuts. But, I don't think I was ever in any real danger.

Back in the day, I never missed a City Council meeting. That was where everybody kinda got together. At one of these meetings was a guy named Vic something. He was one of the people who put me on an assassination list. So, I walked up to him and said in a voice loud enough for everyone in the chambers to hear me, "Hi Vic. I understand I'm on your latest assassination list. Would you give me a bit of a clue before it happens? Let me know right before it happens, will you? I'd kinda like to get my affairs in order."

I thought he was going to fall apart. Everyone in the room was looking at him. Oh my God! He stumbled all over himself as he ran out of the chambers. I was very pleased with myself. Did I just win a battle? I certainly did. Several people came up to me afterwards to offer their support. It was a kick! But, as I said, it wasn't all funny. The police took it somewhat seriously. They didn't have a lot of crimes in Palo Alto, and no public threats to kill people, and yet, a bunch of us were on these assassination lists. One of the names on the lists was Skip Crist, whose law firm had challenged the hippies; going up against the local Venceremos Brigade. I had bought a lot of property that the Venceremos Brigade were living on; where they rented. Unfortunately, it was property that was going to be torn down for the new Palo Alto Medical Research Clinic, so I had to clear them out. Get the Venceremos Brigade off the land. That put me on their assassination list.

So Skip and I, the superintendent of schools and a big heavyset travel agent who was very outspoken and a really good guy, we all went down to the Palo Alto Police Department to meet with Chief William Hydie and one of his lieutenants.

I said "Well, Chief, what do we do? We feel we need protection."

"I gotta tell you, Denny," he said to us, "we can't do anything until something happens to you."

"You mean I've gotta be shot before you can do anything?"

"Yeah. You have to have bodily injury."

We were all kinda shocked. God, how times had changed. This was back in the '60s; a strange time indeed. I said, "Well, can I carry protection?"

The Chief said, "Yes. You all can because you are all on assassination lists and you've all been informed that your life's in danger. Yes, you can carry firearms."

I had a Beretta, which I still have, an engraved Italian Beretta. It's what James Bond carried in the first film, "Dr. No." So anyway, that night I walk in to La Omelette, which was a local hangout run by Frenchmen. Great place. It was where all the young single policemen would hang out trying to pick up girls. These were all guys who started out on the Palo Alto Police Force at the same time I started out in business in 1961. We all got to know each other because we were all young and single. They'd come by when my car would be parked in front of my office and they'd never give me a parking ticket. Instead, they'd pull up, honk on their motorcycle horn and wave and go on. What a great relationship.

There were four of them sitting by the fire when I came over and sat down next to them. One of them said, "My God! There's Denny LeVett. We don't want to get shot." And all of them got up and moved to a different table.

Oh, they thought that was funny. I walked up to them and said, "I demand police protection." They laughed and came back. Then, I said, "No, I don't want to sit with you. You guys are too dangerous." Thinking about it today, it was really funny.

Was I ever really worried about being a target of an assassination? No, I don't think so. I was too young to be smart enough to be worried. Oh sure, at times, on dark streets, or what have you. But more than assassination, I was afraid of shooting my own ass off because I carried the Beretta in my back pocket. I think at the beginning when I was first carrying the Beretta, this caused me more concern, so pretty soon I didn't even carry it anymore.

That was the only time I carried a pistol for protection. And no, I didn't carry a gun when I went to Mexico, as dangerous as it could be. In Mexico, they would shoot you and throw your body in a ditch if you had any sort of a firearm.

Making a Gun Mistake

Even smart people who know guns can make mistakes with them. The most common mistake we hear is, "I didn't know the gun was loaded." As far as I'm concerned, every gun is loaded. But there was a time when I made a mistake with a gun, and while it didn't endanger anyone, it was a stupid thing that I will never forget, and always regret.

It was back in June of '93. I was at dinner at my good friend, Aram Kinosian's house, with a bunch of other pals, including Pete Blackstock. There was a knock on the door. It was a sheriff's deputy. He asked, "Is Mr. LeVett here?"

I came on out and he said, "Mr. LeVett?"

"Well, yes." I said, "And I think I know you. I'm a member of the Sheriff's Advisory Board," which I had been for a long, long while.

He said, "I've got some very bad news for you. Your brother has been found dead."

Oh my God. That explained why we couldn't locate him for two weeks. He'd had a heart attack. That didn't make any sense in my mind, at least the way we sometimes think of things, because he was younger than I was, and he was a schoolteacher. Ironically, the next day in the Sunday *Chronicle*, there was an article on the front page about school teachers in their fifties dropping dead of heart attacks because the cafeteria food was such that it clogged arteries and caused heart attacks. I mean, they explained the whole thing.

My brother was not only a teacher, he was a favorite with students and colleagues alike. One year, he was honored with an award for the #1 Educator in the State of California. He really was loved. His death hit me pretty hard. Anyway, I went out to the back of my house on Del

Ciervo. This was the house that I had bought from Kate and Bill Boyd, and which I eventually sold to Clint Eastwood. It was a Spanish hacienda with eleven bedrooms and two court yards on six-and-a-half-acres, built by the Hollywood director King Vidor in 1918. So, that day I was very emotional. I mean, I had so much guilt because I hadn't seen my brother for awhile. I had gotten angry with him back when I was attempting to get him away from teaching and offered him half interest in the Vagabond's House Inn. I encouraged him to come down to Carmel and operate it. He took a leave of absence and managed it for about three months, and then said, "I don't like this. It's not for me." And that was too bad, because he had a wonderful personality and was so good with people.

What we had done in my family for as long as I could remember was that anytime a member of the family had died, we did a gun salute. I think we fired seven shots. And that's what I did. I went out onto my terrace with a shotgun and fired it seven times.

Yes, that was dumb. Extremely dumb. You can do that in Iowa, but you can't do that in Pebble Beach. It's not like I was near any other houses, but that didn't matter. The shots were heard and a couple of deputies from the sheriff's office came and wanted to arrest me. They put me in the car, and radioed that they were bringing in Dennis LeVett for shooting off a shotgun in the neighborhood; seven shots. But as luck would have it, the same deputy who had come to the front door of Kinosian's, pulled up in his car and told the other deputies, "This is Denny LeVett. He just lost his brother and he's pretty upset."

I tried to explain. "It was a family tradition that we always did a salute. It's a pretty dumb family tradition, now that I think about it, but I was really broken up about my brother dying."

They called the sheriff at that time, Norm Hicks, and one of them said, "Sheriff, we're bringing in Dennis LeVett." Then the other deputy told the sheriff, "His brother just died and we found his brother's body after two weeks in his house. And Mr. LeVett said shooting off the gun was a family tradition. It was a salute to his brother."

The sheriff, thank goodness, said, "Oh, forget it, for God's sake. Let him go. We're not going to arrest him for that."

Later I spoke with the sheriff and thanked him for telling his deputies to let me go. He said, "Denny, you've been such a help to me. You've been great. You have been one of the leading members of the Sheriff's Advisory Board." And he said, "You're a gun collector, I can't believe that you don't have a concealed weapon permit."

I told him, "You know, I've never really felt that I needed one, and I never felt very comfortable walking around carrying a gun. I don't need to have a gun on me."

Anyway, that was a dumb-ass thing for me to do at the time, even though I was overwhelmed with grief because of my brother Bill.

The Dream

It's perhaps because Pierre, the capital of South Dakota, is a city of fewer than 14,000 people that so many Americans are unfamiliar with its interesting history. Oh, and first of all, its pronunciation, which is *not* like the French version of Peter (pee-YAYER) but is a homonym for a boat dock, like a *pier* (peer). Anyway, Pierre is as far as the French got down the Missouri River. You might remember from your American history class that the French controlled much of what became the American Midwest and sold the land to us as the Louisiana Purchase in 1803. That didn't mean much to the French settlers in the area, since they didn't recognize the Americans, but some thirty years later when some American army troops persuaded the French to accept the inevitable and find other places to live, they finally understood. Fort Pierre, was named after an American fur trader from St. Louis; Pierre Chouteau. It was built as a military and trading post in 1832 by John Jacob Astor's American Fur Company and became one of the most important trading centers in the northern Great Plains.

That didn't mean that the area was tamed. Far from it. Ft. Pierre, on the west side of the river and the city of Pierre on the east were targets of river pirates who would arrive on boats and rafts in the middle of the night to pillage, murder, and rape. And that's the reason for recounting this story.

For me, it started as a dream . . . literally. It was in 1971, but I have to go back another ten years when I first came to Palo Alto, in 1961, to start my career. I was an antique gun collector and excited to discover that Portuguese Hall in nearby Mountain View had a gun show every Saturday. And I have to tell you, it was a pretty darn enterprising and successful gun show. I got to meet all sorts of people and everybody I met there I'm still doing business with today. People like Mitch Luksich, Greg Martin, Pete Buckston, and others; some of the great characters.

Greg Martin was the biggest name, even back then. We were the same age exactly; both 22. But this guy had more street smarts than anybody I'd ever met in my life. I first met Greg in 1959 at his parents' Chicken Kitchen in San Martin, California. San Martin was founded by his grandfather Martin Murphy, who built the first Catholic church in the southern part of Santa Clara County.

As you drove by on Highway 101 (it was only two lanes then), you'd see their signs outside: "Best chicken you ever had" and "Famous Chicken Kitchen," and then there was another sign that read, "We buy and sell antique guns." Not even antique firearms; antique guns. Naturally, I had to stop and take a look and that's how I met Greg. By the way, he is still one of my best friends today. We still do business together.

A year or so after we met, Greg returned with his van from a trip to northern Mexico. Now, in those days, who took their van through Mexico trying to buy antique guns, going into Guadalajara, Ciudad Obregon, and San Angelo? Well, Greg did. And there was this wonderful town that was an old silver city called Alamos. I have landed there a number of times. In Alamos, Greg bought out the arsenal. Alamos was at one time an old wild west Mexican town and it was one of the silver capitals of the world. The great domes of silver made many men rich, which explained why this small town had a pretty big *policia*.

So Greg visited the police, went to several parties in the area, met a few politicians, and was told he could buy any of the antique guns out of the armory or out of the police station that he wanted. He bought hundreds of guns, not just there, but all over Mexico.

But here it was, the morning after he got back, which was Saturday morning, at the Mountain View gun show. He was selling guns out of the back of his van. I picked out a couple of old relic types, a Winchester rifle, and some single-action pistols. This one particular single-action was a very early one; from 1873. It was the Colt single-action .45 marked "U.S." on the side. As the story goes, these guns were delivered to the soldiers of the United States Army and the 7th Cavalry Regiment who fought at Little Big Horn; Custer's "Last Stand" in June of 1876. The gun I picked up was an artillery model and it was well worn. On its walnut grips, it had initials carved in Indian signage. These Indian decorations on the grips were very crude. When I picked it up, this gun felt particularly good to me. I cocked it and released the hammer again and again. I twirled it a few times. It felt so good to me. I loved this gun. I think I paid Greg $125 for it.

As time went on, this became my favorite gun. And not to sound kooky or so involved with a love for firearms, but it was something of an obsession. I had a connection with this gun unlike any I had had with any other gun, before or since. I kept it on my coffee table. I'd pick it up, cock it, let the hammer down. It just felt so darned good. I decided this was a gun I would never part with.

As a matter of fact, some experts examined it, because it was pre-Custer, U.S. Cavalry, and they were sure it was a scout's gun, an Indian scout's gun. That could explain the Indian markings on the grip. Or not. It very well could have been picked up on the Custer battlefield by an Indian, who made it his personal gun and marked the grips.

The night of the dream was right after my grandfather died, and I had been going through some pretty serious internal conflicts, reviewing issues and upsets in my life. I was living at the Laning Chateau then, a building I owned in Palo Alto, and I was having a hard time sleeping. This particular night was one of those nights, when even a sleeping aid didn't work. I went to bed at 10:30pm, or quarter to 11:00, and right before I went to sleep, I was sitting on the edge of my bed with this wonderful Colt .45 single-action Army in my hand, thinking about the gun and how strange it was, this thing I had for this gun. *Whatever*, as they say, I finally put the gun down and went off to nigh-nigh land, sugarplums, and the like. And here's where it gets interesting. Or *strange*, however you want to see it. It was something I can't explain. I can only guess, and maybe I'm wrong, but I swear to you, I think I spent most of that night reliving a period of time that had to have been during another lifetime. It was so vivid, so real, so personal that I can't explain it any other way. It is still so real to me that more than 40 years later, I can remember exactly where I was. I can even remember the conversations that took place in the dream. Now, I *call* it a dream, but that's for lack of any other explanation. In fact, it was much more than a dream, because I felt so fully alive in what was happening. Sights, sounds, smells, feelings. Oh, it was much, much more than a dream.

What I remember first in the dream was that I was suddenly awakened by a pounding on my door. I got out of my bed and was thinking to myself, "Where the hell am I?" Now understand, this was all while I was asleep, but I thought I was awake. I didn't get out of my bed really—not the one in my bedroom in the Laning Chateau in 1971, that is. Instead, I was on the second story of a building with dirt streets outside. Now, I knew where I was. I was this character that I must have been in an earlier life. Yes, I certainly did know where I was, and who I was. I was the sheriff of this town and also a shopkeeper and I lived above my shop. I guess I was single, because I didn't have anybody else living with me.

The pounding continued at my door. It was a group of townspeople shouting, "We're being attacked! We're being attacked by pirates!" So this sets the time as the late 1880s or early 1890s. This is when river boats and packet boats were being attacked by pirates up and down the Missouri river where it joins the Mississippi all the way up into South Dakota. This problem was very serious because the pirates also attacked small towns along the river, defended by armed guards. But for some reason, in my dream, this town where I was didn't worry about pirates, because it had, I guess, a pretty competent sheriff. It had a lot of ranchers, and some fairly wealthy ranchers at that. I guess we kinda felt impervious. I don't know why. The name of this town was Ft. Pierre. But I'm getting ahead of myself. In my dream, I wasn't thinking about the name of the town because Pierre was where I lived.

The townspeople were in a state of panic, as you might understand, because we were being attacked by pirates. I was yelling out the window, "Arm yourselves! Arm yourselves! We must defend the town!"

I went to my dresser and pulled open the bottom drawer—I remember this so vividly it's amazing—and there was my gun belt and this trusty .45 single-action. I strapped it on and went outside into the street.

I was on the main street of town; there were stores on both sides. The street ran down to the Missouri River. There were warehouses on either side of the street. This was a very prosperous area because we were kind of the last outpost; on the west side of the Missouri River was nothing but the Wild West. The east side was civilization, very close to Iowa and Minnesota. That is, civilization maybe not as we know it today, but civilization as they knew it back then. For a half-century this had been a major trading center between the western frontier and civilized America to the east.

Anyway, one of the warehouses was on fire, and by the light of the fire, I could see several boats near the wharf. What we needed to do was to repel those pirates who had come to our town in those boats. I'm not kidding. This really happened in those days. And it was kinda like we knew it would happen sooner or later to this wonderful town of ours. I don't know why we weren't better prepared.

In my dream, as I was running down to the river, I saw this huge beautiful mansion on the left-hand side (I can still picture it today). It was a large Edwardian mansion, all wood with a full-length front porch. This must have been in early November. It seemed like Indian Summer. But the reason I feel it was early November is that there was isinglass on the porch, and they didn't put the isinglass on (which to me always looked like waxed paper), until it was really time for snow.

There were people running all over. There was gunfire. I was trying to lead some townsmen over towards the wharf, to the banks of the river to fire upon the pirates. But then I heard screams coming from the mansion and I saw people running. Through the isinglass, I was seeing these images. These were people, real people. I heard another scream and then I heard gunfire.

I raised my gun, that wonderful U.S. Army Colt .45 single-action, and I fired at this person behind the isinglass and hit him. Of course, the first thing that came to my mind was: Should I have done that? Who did I hit? Did I hit a pirate or did I hit somebody that lived in the house?

I was thinking, How dumb of me. Who did I hit? This worried me. But I must have hit one of the pirates because they were yelling, "Let's find him and get him. Let's find out who it was," and they ran across the length of the porch to the front door.

Suddenly, I froze in my tracks and realized, "Oh, my God. They're after me!" I never felt so terrified in my entire life. I had the sense to realize that I couldn't get away with all of them about to run out the front to the street, so I jumped into a window box, and without breaking the glass, I kicked the frame open and slid through to the basement below. Then I closed the window.

I was in the dark and I could see them outside searching for me, running around, yelling, "Where is he?" As far as they were concerned, it could have been anybody, because there were a lot of people all running around and they didn't seem to think it was any one of them.

Somehow in my mind, I was convinced that they were going to find me and do me in. As courageous a man as I thought I was, as much a man of adventure that I thought I was, I never felt such a panic in my life. I never ever felt that my life was so in danger, and I was terrified. I was holding my breath because I didn't want anybody to hear me breathing. I didn't want to make a sound.

There were pirates running around and two of them stood outside the window box. I was thinking that I must have shot somebody important. Maybe one of the leaders of the pirates because they were intent on finding me.

It was probably only a couple of minutes, but it seemed like forever. I was down in the basement and I was talking to myself; not out loud, but as internal conversation. I spurred myself on and began to regain my composure. I could feel my courage return. I repeatedly told myself that I must regain my honor. I remember this so well.

With that, I crawled out of the window box with my pistol in my hand, telling myself I was ready to face the world. At this point, you'd better believe I was ready to take on the pirates because I was so ashamed of myself for hiding in the basement. I could see that down at the wharf the townspeople were repelling the pirates, so with my new-found courage, which every sheriff should have, I ran into the mansion. It was bedlam, with lots of screaming and crying and there was a pirate's body on the floor. I knew it was the one I had shot because he fell right at the spot where I shot at him.

Then I ran out of the house and down to the wharf where I joined my fellow townspeople in repelling the rest of the pirates. I remember feeling so proud of the town, and that we were all proud of ourselves. The next thing I knew, the sun was coming up. We were counting our wounded and assessing the damage, what had burned down. (I never did see the wealthy owner of the mansion in my dream.) But what I do remember was everybody congratulating each other and feeling proud that we had repelled the enemy and the townspeople had won. And this was no rinky-dink little boat of pirates—this was a couple of barges of pirates. I looked down at my Army .45, and I thought, "I will never part with this gun." There were lots of hugs and congratulations. We went to what looked like the downstairs level of my store. Everybody came in for coffee and it was one of these very proud moments. The parts of the story that I remember in detail were the beginning and the middle. The end was just more back-slapping over our victory.

After the dream was over, I woke up in my bed in the Laning Chateau. It was about 6:30 in the morning. Fully awake, I realized that I had experienced something that wasn't just a dream. I had experienced the pirate attack in reality. Call it what you may, but I had relived a segment of my past life. I hadn't experienced life as more real than what happened to me that night in my dream. But it seemed so strange, so indefinable, that I didn't tell anyone about it. I didn't want people to think that I was cuckoo. Especially in my business, people expect to be working with someone who is level-headed; not someone who is having flashbacks of a past life.

Then a number of years ago, I was flying my Cessna over the area that I was sure was where the "dream" had been set. I was convinced it was Nebraska, convinced, and I flew back and forth, searching up and down, looking for this town. I knew that it was on the west shore because I remember the sun coming up that morning from over the river. It was the west shore of the Missouri. No question in my mind. I could not remember the name of the town, but I certainly remembered the buildings and the wide street that went down to the river.

If you walked down to the end of the street, you would walk into the Missouri River. I searched up and down the Missouri River and didn't find the town. I don't know why, but in my mind I "knew" it had to be in Nebraska. I even searched the towns in Missouri, even though I was sure that it had to be Nebraska. Why it couldn't be South Dakota, I don't know.

Then I happened to meet a young woman who had graduated from the University of South Dakota and who was familiar with much of the history of the area, especially towns along the Missouri River. She and I drove around for a couple of days, exploring towns along the river and some of the Sioux Indian reservations. Mostly I was following the river, heading north. I was crossing over to the west side when I could.

I finally got up to Pierre, the capital of South Dakota, and across the river was Ft. Pierre. We drove across a bridge and now we were on the west side of the Missouri River. When we got into that town, I tell you I recognized it. Ft. Pierre is an old town, but even though most of the buildings were newer than I remembered from that night, I still saw a lot that was familiar to me. The way I figured it, the man I was back then — the sheriff — could have lived another thirty or forty years, or even more. My memory from that one dream was from maybe the late 1880s or early 1890s. It was certainly plausible that the sheriff could have lived into the 1930s and had seen some of the buildings that were still standing today.

We got out and walked around town, including along the main street. I had the shock of my life when I discovered that the main street went all the way to the Missouri River. I walked down the main street, and I knew that this was it. This was the town.

This was a Sunday and the local museum was open. There I saw historical photographs of the town from my dream, including my own building, which was where I had the shop. It was akin to a general store and I lived above it. That building no longer existed, but the photographs were perfectly clear. I saw the downstairs in the shop where everybody had coffee that morning, and the pot-belly stove. I was looking at photographs of people in the store who were identified in the captions by name. I was reading the names, and lo and behold, there was the name of Clyde Strutz. My grandfather on my mother's side was named Strutz! I was standing there looking at this photograph of a man with my grandfather's name and I said out loud, "I don't believe this. I don't believe it." This is Clyde Strutz.

I remembered my grandfather telling me that he had an uncle, and he might have referred to him as Uncle Clyde. I don't know. But he had an uncle who went to South Dakota. I don't recall that he ever went to see him there, but anyway, I was convinced that Clyde Strutz was my grandfather's uncle, and therefore my great-great uncle. So it wasn't my past life, but great-uncle Clyde's life that I experienced in that dream. Or maybe Clyde Strutz came back as me, but I don't think that was the case. I really can't explain how the dream could have been so vivid if I hadn't been there. Do dreams or images transfer from one person to another? I've never heard of that before. I don't know what happened, but I know what I experienced . . . in my "dream."

This final note . . . when I woke up from that dream, the gun was right there on the table where I had put it down the night before so that I could reach it from the bed and pick it up. No, it wasn't loaded. You don't shoot antiques like that. But, I will say that to this day, I look at it and say, "I will never part with this gun."

A Gun Lover's Story

I'm a Life Member of the National Rifle Association. I've been a member for sixty years. I've gone hunting on more than one occasion with some of the top brass of the NRA. We are all on a first-name basis. But that doesn't mean I'm lockstep with their policies. Not by a long shot, so to speak.

I grew up on a farm in Iowa and started getting interested in guns when I was nine years old, under the watchful eye of my grandfather. I never was an ardent hunter. I shot one rabbit. I couldn't sleep. Cried. Prayed that I would be forgiven. Never shot another rabbit again. Shot a squirrel one day. Same thing. Never ever shot a squirrel again. After some of those conflicts with myself, I never shot animals again. Birds, yes, but pheasants, only pheasants.

Over the years, I bought, sold, and traded guns as both a hobby, and as a source of revenue. I had become very knowledgeable about guns, in part from the influx of weapons that were brought back to the States by returning veterans of the war against the Nazis; from Lugers and Walthers to Belgium Brownings and Thompson submachine guns.

There was a time during the Fifties when I was rounding up guns to send to the rebels in Cuba who were in a valiant struggle to overthrow the brutal Fulgencio Batista. We all believed that Batista was the worst dictator there could ever be and that the savior was Castro. I think even the State Department thought that for a while. Of course, Castro subsequently fell out of favor with many of his supporters, including me, but at the time, it was indeed a noble cause.

I continue to live in the gun world to this day, attending gun shows and buying, selling, and trading guns; having accumulated one of the finest collection of Colt Paterson firearms in the world, including an impressive array of Philadelphia Derringers, among others.

At a major gun show in Las Vegas in September of 2011, before the slaughters in the Aurora, Colorado movie theater, and the Newtown, Connecticut school, I presented a proposal to NRA officials that I believed would help get guns out of the hands of people who were mentally ill. I also pointed out to them that if they took leadership on this issue, it would get the biggest public relations boost they could ever imagine. But their response was that trying to define who shouldn't have guns because they were mentally unbalanced "would open up a can of worms."

I wasn't happy with their answer. I am like the great majority of NRA members who believe that the executives at the top of the organization need to set out a more rational policy for gun ownership in the United States. Also, I strongly assert that no one needs to have a fully-automatic firearm or an assault weapon, or magazines that hold more than ten bullets, or armor-piercing "cop-killer" bullets.

While I don't like the idea of registering all guns, I do believe that there should be a system of background checks, so that guns aren't sold to people who shouldn't have them; like felons, people under court order, and those with mental problems. I quickly adopted an idea proposed by a friend, Randy Charles, that a database be established to include people who have been vetted and shown to be safe gun owners; much like TSA-PRE that is in place for frequent flyers, thereby eliminating the need to go through airport searches every time one boards a plane. For these people, there wouldn't need to be the delay that could occur with required background checks.

From the conversations I've had with friends, I believe I represent the thinking of the modern gun owner, as well as of many people who don't own firearms. We agree that while guns are part of American history and contemporary culture, there should be limits on who has access to firearms. We need laws and proper enforcement to ensure that those who would be dangerous to others and to themselves, should be prevented from possessing a gun. It would be crazy to think otherwise.

POLITICS

Nothing is Certain in Politics

This anecdote begins as a California political story and ends up at the White House. But actually, I'll start it off in Europe when I was on a skiing trip in the resort towns of Cortina, Italy, and St. Moritz, Switzerland, with *The Wild Turkeys*. The Wild Turkeys were a group of friends who did things together; Ronny and Jack Faia, Merv Sutton, Chris Tescher, Aram Kinosian, Don Burnett, and yours truly. Our motto now is "We're no longer wild, we're just turkeys!"

But back to California for a moment . . . since I was president of the Lincoln Club of Northern California, I was involved in the 2002 gubernatorial race. We were all certain that Richard Riordan, the former mayor of Los Angeles, would win the Republican nomination for governor and go up against the incumbent, Gray Davis. Riordan was a solid, moderate Republican whose primary competition was William Simon Jr., the son of the former U.S. Treasury Secretary, William Simon, who I knew as a fellow Colt Paterson collector.

Anyway, young Simon didn't have a prayer. He was a relatively unknown Right Wing Republican, and not a particularly good campaigner. At the time I left for Europe, two weeks before the election, Riordan was up 40% over Simon, as he should have been, since Riordan was the Republican poster boy; the guy who could beat Davis. Everybody knew Riordan was going to win. I had held several big parties; meet-and-greet fundraisers in my house for Riordan. All my political buddies were on a first-name basis with him. I'd get calls from him asking favors—can you deliver this, can you do that, or I've got a speech in San Jose; would you introduce me, and so on.

Anyway, back to Europe . . . my train left St. Moritz at

eleven o'clock in the morning for Zurich, where we were all staying overnight. It was the day after the election. I boarded the train and this beautiful woman was sitting across from me. She had an English edition of the *Herald Tribune* and on the front of the *Tribune* was a picture of William Simon Jr. that caught my attention. Since he didn't have a prayer in the election, what was his picture doing on the front of the *Herald Tribune*?

I shouted, "What!" And I snatched the paper away. "I don't believe it! I don't believe it!"

The woman said, most calmly and in perfect English, "Apparently you're from California and this was not your candidate." It turned out that she was the wife of the president of Deutsche Bank; they had a home in St. Moritz and she was just returning to Germany.

Oh my God! Absolute shock! I was repeating, "This is impossible." She was smiling gracefully.

I apologized profusely for grabbing her newspaper. "I am so sorry. I've never done that before in my life and I'll never do it again. I am so shocked because I'm president of the Lincoln Club and I left the States thinking that our candidate—not this guy, was safe. There's no way he could be beaten. Our man was 40% ahead of Simon," I said, poking at the picture on the front page. So much for a sure thing!

I called Duf Sundheim, my successor at the Lincoln Club who was now president. It was maybe three o'clock in the morning in Palo Alto, California. So Duf answers the phone, and I said, "Duf, I'm sorry to call you at this hour. I can't believe it. I'm on a train leaving St. Moritz. I just saw the *Herald Tribune* and it shows Simon as the winner."

"Yeah, Denny," he said.

"Duf, what happened? What in the hell happened? How in the hell did this possibly happen?"

He said, "Riordan didn't try very hard these last couple of weeks and was slipping in the polls. I guess the soccer moms thought he was a shoo-in and didn't get out the vote for him. It was the worst turn-out you ever saw." For heaven's sake, Riordan didn't even carry Los Angeles County. But there are no do-overs, so here was Simon running for governor against the very unpopular Gray Davis. Simon had no chance of being elected because he was too far right wing. I just spent three years as Chairman of the Lincoln Club of Northern California trying to move my fellow Republicans to the middle of the road. That was the only way we were going to get a candidate elected, and Duf Sundheim agreed with me. When he became Chairman of the California Republican Party, he did exactly that. He moved us to the middle of the road, got backing and raised our visibility. But that was later.

Anyway, after the primary, the Bush White House sent out invitations. They want five of the leading Republicans in the State of California to come back for a breakfast with the President. How they got my name as a lead Republican in the State of California, I don't know; somebody bamboozled somebody. But there I was with Jerry Parsky from Los Angeles, Fred Lowell, and Duf Sundheim and Tom Stephenson, a venture capitalist from Menlo Park who was the head of Sequoia Capital, and a very active, very close friend of George W. Bush. Tom was also a pretty good friend of mine.

The five of us had a great breakfast. The President couldn't make it. It was seven o'clock in the morning; he probably wasn't even up yet. Instead it was Dick Cheney and Karl Rove, the Vice President, and the Chief White House Political Advisor that attended. The breakfast room was in this underground bunker. It was phenomenal, down below the White House right under the Oval Office. Navy guards watched over us. We were served the classic shit-on-a-shingle, if you'll pardon my language, but it was the best chipped beef and gravy I've ever had in my life.

Cheney apologized that the President couldn't make it that morning and said the reason we were there was that they needed to know how to get Simon elected governor of California. They said, "This is something the President wants more than anything; for Simon to be elected. Mr. LeVett, you're first."

I said bluntly, "You can't get him elected in California. First off, you have to understand the state. It's like none of the other forty-nine states. California is unto itself and you can't crack it. You cannot be a right-wing, religious conservative, or any conservative Republican, and win in California. You can't. If you think you can, then show me."

I added, "Simon is not well known to the general public. Only conservatives know him really well. His father, William Simon Sr., was well respected, and as a matter of fact, in the introduction of my book, *The Paterson Colt Book*, I've got a salute to William Simon. But you can't get his son elected. I couldn't even begin to tell you how to go about it."

The person on my left was Fred Lowell, who's a brilliant strategist and the political guru of Pillsbury, Madison & Sutro, a West Coast version of an East Coast "white-shoe" law firm. He was the head of their political department and a good guy. Fred Lowell put it simply, "I can't add a thing to what Denny had to say. He's absolutely right. There is no way you're going to get Simon elected."

Then Tom was next. He was a very artful speaker. "You know, we've got to admit that Gray Davis is not popular. Riordan could have beaten Davis because Riordan is essentially a Democrat in Republican clothes, but he was beaten by the Right Wing of the party. He was a sure thing to beat Gray Davis. Simon can't do it."

Everybody around the table, all of us from California, were nodding our heads in agreement. There was nothing that could be done. So the conversation shifted. This was six months after the 9/11 attack, and we spent the next hour or so talking about terrorism in America. All in all, it was a very interesting discussion.

Simon, beset by major business scandals, since went on to loose the General Election to Gray Davis.

Tom Campbell

My political career has mostly been as a man behind the scenes. As an active member of the Lincoln Club in Northern California, in 1988, we were searching for a candidate for the U. S. House of Representatives representing the 14th Congressional District that included the Palo Alto area. Tom Ford, who was the founder of the Lincoln Club in Northern California, and just a brilliant guy, announced that he had found a professor of law and economics from Stanford; a very brilliant young man he thought might be interested in running for congress in our very moderate to liberal district.

Tom Campbell was in the State Senate at the time and he took a leave of absence to run. First he edged out freshman Congressman Ernie Konnyu, a Republican, in the primary, and then got by Democrat Anna Eshoo, much to the surprise of many of the pundits. Tom was so attractive and well-spoken, in an educated district that prized intellect and articulation, that he was able to pull off a win in an area that had a definite Democratic tinge. In fact, Tom Campbell was the most attractive candidate the Lincoln Club could possibly have. We were so proud. George Shultz, Secretary of State under President Reagan and a major political figure in California, stated publicly that Tom Campbell was one of the ten most intelligent men in Washington, D.C. Of course, being so bright didn't fly everywhere, as we were to find later.

When Pete Wilson, who was in the U.S. Senate at the time, decided to run for governor, and won, he had to appoint someone to take his seat. Logically, we in the Lincoln Club of Northern California were all pushing for Tom Campbell. He wasn't the choice of the people in the southern part of the state, but certainly Central and

Northern California rallied behind Tom. I had a very good rapport with the new governor and talked to Pete a number of times. I even made a trip to Sacramento to discuss Tom Campbell, and Pete was very receptive. Tom Campbell, himself, also spent a lot of time with Pete. He was planning to go to Russia for Christmas where his wife was teaching, but cancelled because his wife, Susanne, felt he should be in California to press his case.

I got a phone call from Tom right before Christmas. He said, "Denny, I just got a call from Pete Wilson, and he said, 'I can't say too much Tom, but I'll say enough to give you confidence. Go spend Christmas with your wife. Be back by January 1st." Tom continued, "I'm headed for Russia to see Susanne, and it really looks good, Denny. In so many words, Pete said I had the nomination."

All of us who knew the situation and were promoting Tom were pleased as Christmas punch. We knew that Pete's short list was Tom Campbell, first, and Condoleezza Rice, second. Tom made much more sense because he had great credentials and more experience in Washington. Pete Wilson naturally spent his Christmases down in his home area of California, which was in the southland, Orange County. People like Don Bren, who had the Irvine Company, a private real estate investment company in Los Angeles, was one of Pete's closest supporters. It turned out that the Orange County Republicans spent the Christmas holidays with Pete Wilson and convinced him to choose John Seymour as his replacement in the Senate. Against his own judgment, he later said. "This was the last thing I had in my mind. Seymour was the most valuable negotiator I had in the state legislature."

It was a shock to all of us. Of course, we all knew John Seymour, an ex-real estate broker who became a state senator. He was the minority whip and very powerful in his own right. Tom got the message on January 2nd, and called me. "Denny, he picked John Seymour."

It was such a big mistake. If Pete had put Tom in the

Senate, he'd still be there today. Once in office, he would have shown his intelligence and won re-election easily. And oh, what a difference it would have been to have him in the United States Senate. He certainly would have been far more important to the country and the state than Dianne Feinstein, who easily beat Seymour in the special election in 1992. She probably wouldn't have run against Tom, but if she had, she would have lost. He was that good.

I think about it all the time. I think about how stupid I was not to stay on Pete throughout the holidays. Pete knew it was a mistake, too. The night he left Sacramento, after his run as governor was over, he stopped off at a dinner with Duncan Matteson and me in Palo Alto. So there we were having dinner and having a grand old time, and Pete looked at Duncan and me and said, "I'm pretty happy with the job I did, but I made one huge glaring mistake. Denny, you know what that was?"

I said, "Yeah, Pete. I know what it was, but I don't want to say what it was because I may be wrong. It may be something else."

Pete said, "Well, the huge mistake I made was that I should've picked Tom Campbell or Condoleezza Rice. I thought it was a little early maybe, for Condoleezza Rice, because I knew she was growing in the political scene, but it was perfect timing for Tom Campbell. That was a huge, blaring mistake."

This was a real "domino-effect" year of the Republicans. We had Alan Cranston's seat coming up again in a special election for Seymour's seat, and we had Tom Campbell going to run for it against Bruce Herschensohn in the primary. When there were tough decisions to be made, it was expected that Tom would consult with the half-dozen of us in his kitchen cabinet. I think Duncan was one of the group, and Tom Ford, and a couple of the Lincoln Clubbers.

So, one day I get a phone call from Karen Keane. Karen was a member of the Lincoln Club and on Tom Campbell's Congressional staff in Washington. But, I'm going to back up just one quick second—Matt Little, who's very influential here in Carmel, an insurance broker, a devoted Republican and a member of the Lincoln Club, marched into my office one day, and said, "Denny, okay, you're a good buddy. I've donated $1,000 to Tom Campbell and I want my money back."

I asked him, "Matt what are you talking about?"

He said, "A bill came up in Congress that prohibits hunting on federal grounds. Now, I'm going to tell you something. Since before the Revolutionary War and the Declaration of Independence, we've all had a right to hunt on federal grounds, obeying the hunting laws, of course, but we all have that right, and this bill that prohibits regular Americans from hunting on federal grounds is the most odious bill that's ever come up. All of us that are hunters hunt on federal land. It's not only a God-given right, but a constitutional right to hunt on federal grounds. Tom Campbell was the only Republican that voted for it, along with a bunch of Democrats, and I want my money back. I'm not going to vote for him for U.S. Senator."

I picked up the phone. I called Tom and I said, "Tom, I don't think this was very smart. It is a right that all of us feel we have; to hunt on federal grounds. Why would you vote against that?"

"Oh God, Denny," Tom said, "I don't like guns. I don't like hunting. I guess I wasn't informed."

"Well, I don't expect you to pick up the phone and call me very often, except when there is something that is touchy like that."

He said, "I didn't know it was touchy. I just thought, 'Well, yeah, federal grounds, we can't have the whole nation hunting on federal grounds.'"

"Okay. Tom, please be aware."

Then a couple of weeks later, I get that call from Karen Keane. She said, "Denny, have I got good news. This morning, Tom got an endorsement from Sarah Brady. Isn't that the greatest news in the world?"

I said, "Karen, excuse me, I'm having chest pains. I know you're from Massachusetts, and very anti-guns, and that's fine because that is probably one of the most liberal states in the country, but Karen, we're talking about Tom running for the United States Senate from California, *not* Massachusetts. This is the west. People have guns. Whatever you do, you've got to get rid of that endorsement. I think it's the most dangerous thing that could happen to Tom."

Then I called Tom and said, "Tom, we all know your stance on gun control. I want to tell you that if gun control was on the ballot today, it would lose huge. It'd lose by 75%. There's something you've got to understand, Tom, and that is that San Francisco is very liberal, very anti-gun and so is Palo Alto. But you set one foot out of the cities and you're in the country, and those people will fight to keep their guns."

I told him, "This may be how you feel, but say it some other way. I'm against Saturday night specials. I'm against assault rifles. You can't say you're against the Second Amendment of the Constitution of United States. The same is true on abortion. You lose 50% of the votes if you say you're pro-choice. You lose 50% of the votes if you say you're pro-life. Come up with something else."

I had come up with a better line when I was talking with Dan Lungren when he was running for governor. He was Catholic, and he was very anti-abortion. I told him he didn't have to say, "I'm pro-life." I told him to shut up. "Don't lecture everybody on this subject. Don't do it. Just say that *'The choice is in the home. I think it has to do with family.'* Leave it at that and you're not going to lose votes."

Okay, getting back to Tom Campbell. He said, "Well, Denny, maybe you are right. Maybe, I better rethink this, but I thought it would be very exciting."

I said, "Tom, it could lose you the election. Right now, you're 20 some points ahead in the polls, but you could probably lose the election over something like this."

That same day, that very same day, we got word that Sonny Bono had thrown his hat into the ring to run for the

Republican nomination for the Cranston seat. Word came out that Sonny Bono was paid $300,000 to get into the race. It had been set up by George Bush, Sr., (he was President Bush, then), along with the far right religious conservatives in Orange County, who wanted Herschensohn. They knew that Bono would take votes away from Tom, and that Herschensohn would beat Barbara Boxer. And that's what happened. It was a real scandal. Sonny Bono was hired to hurt Tom, and when the ballots were counted, Bono pulled 417,000 votes, which gave the nomination to Herschensohn. Herschensohn also played dirty against Tom, putting out a flyer that Tom was a sheep in wolf's clothing, a far left liberal. Of course that wasn't true, but people believed it, and they had a choice if they didn't like Herschensohn—they could vote for Bono.

And if that wasn't enough, there were the Rodney King riots in Los Angeles. The riots were the scariest thing that could happen. There was something like 100,000 applications for guns over the next few days in the Los Angeles area. With Tom's anti-gun statements and the Sarah Brady endorsement, his poll numbers went from 20 points ahead down to about a half-a-point ahead on Election Day.

So yes, Herschensohn beat Tom, and in November, Boxer beat Herschensohn by a half-million votes. She won more than half the votes of Republican women who couldn't stand the right-wing Herschensohn. But you have to know that Boxer wouldn't have beaten Tom Campbell. I still think that if Tom had consulted with his kitchen cabinet before he took some of the positions that he did, he could have beaten Herschensohn. Not that he should have taken positions he didn't believe in. Just that he should have *explained them differently*, so he wouldn't offend the Republican base. Anyway, dear Tom Campbell, I felt very sad for you. I wish you had won.

Flying with Barbara Boxer

It was back in 2001. We had just gotten George W. Bush elected, and I was President of the Lincoln Club. Proud of it then, before we knew what Bush and Cheney would do. I had been skiing in St. Moritz and had just flown in from Zurich to Washington, D.C., where I could make a connection back to San Francisco.

I was on a United Boeing 757, which is the one that had the large First Class section. I was seated next to the bulkhead, feeling just terrible because I'd picked up an awful cold. I discovered that my seat mate was a dwarf-like creature, slouched in her seat with her shoes off and her feet up against the bulkhead. Her dress was up around her thighs, but I wasn't really looking. Anyway, I'm thinking that even though she could afford to sit in first class, she certainly is not acting like she belonged there.

Being the gracious fellow that I always try to be, and feeling ill, I said to this woman, "I'm sorry. I've been skiing in St. Moritz, and I've come down with a doozy of a cold. I will try my best to not cough so that it might disturb you."

To tell you how sick I was and how blurred my vision was, I hadn't noticed that the woman sitting next to me was California's Junior Senator, Barbara Boxer. It wasn't until I noticed that she was reading the *Congressional Record* that I hazily put together who she was. I was acquainted with Senator Boxer, having met her a number of times at social and political events, so I decided to have some fun. I said, "Oh. I see you are reading the Congressional Record. Are you in Congress?"

"No," she said haughtily, "I'm not in Congress. I'm in the U.S. Senate."

I said, "Well, my head's hurting and my vision is kinda

195

funny, but I'm pretty sure you're not Dianne Feinstein. You aren't, are you?"

She just about erupted. "No, I'm not Dianne Feinstein. I'm Barbara Boxer."

Keeping a straight face, I said, "Oh for heaven's sake, then you're in the Senate."

I was having too much fun, and it kinda went on from there for a while. I don't remember the rest of it, but she was nice enough to help me with my cold. She got up and retrieved some cold medicine from her carry-on bag.

Later, during the course of our chatting, because it was evident that I knew so much about politics, she asked, "So who are you?"

And I said, "I'm Denny LeVett."

She replied, "Oh, that name is familiar."

I said, "Yes, we've met."

She was having fun with me now and repeated, "That name is familiar."

I raised my eyebrows and said, "Well, that could be. I'm the Chairman and President of the Lincoln Club in Northern California." And boy, did that shut her up.

Bush League

I was made President-Elect of the Lincoln Club of Northern California, and when the President, Fred Lowell, had an aneurysm and became ill, I kinda took over the leadership about a year early. Back in 1998, I was asked to introduce George W. Bush, who was trying to make up his mind whether or not he would run for the Presidency of the United States. On a Saturday night he was to be speaking at Pepperdine, a good Republican University, and then stay the night at Pebble Beach, where he was speaking before the Lincoln Club the next morning.

On Saturday, I gave him a heck of an introduction, I must say, with lots of humor. And I think he gave one of the best speeches I ever heard him give. Even to this day. He had a kinda Paul Newman look and feel, and everybody was just thrilled to death. They thought he definitely was going to be our candidate, which of course, he was. Standing ovation.

After the speech was over, George W. said to me, "Denny," he called me Denny, "that was one of the best introductions I ever had, and I want to tell you something, I want to use you all I can—for introductions. The humor, the clarity, the energy, it was great."

Well, I felt very proud. Then, of course, I became President of the Lincoln Club and he became our Republican nominee for President of the United States, so I had many other opportunities to introduce him at different rallies throughout the State. Now you would think with the comments he made to me, he would be pleased to see me, but the truth was that he never remembered my face or my name. I found this kinda interesting, because, with all due humility, people usually remember my face, or my name, or both. I am lucky that way, I guess.

But with W, it frustrated the hell out of me. He would look right at me and not recognize me. He'd pass by me and not even say "hi" to me. And here I was, feeling I had a reasonably important position in Northern California Republican politics. At that time the Lincoln Club was probably the most active go-to Republican Club in Northern California, maybe the State. Because what we were doing was looking for candidates. We didn't just back one candidate or pick a couple of candidates and back them. We went out to *find* good candidates (like Tom Campbell).

So, it should be no surprise that I lost a little enthusiasm for W. Part of it was because I felt slighted by his ignoring me, and also because I wondered if he had his act together. He didn't recognize me, even after we had been at the same podium a number of times where I had introduced him. That was a little strange to me.

Then in the late summer of 2000, probably early September, we were getting down to election time. W was doing a whistle stop through California and one of the stops was in Salinas, an agricultural center and the Monterey County seat. I organized every Republican office holder in Monterey County, Santa Cruz County, San Benito County, and so on, to be there. Local and county officials, plus the Republican legislators in Sacramento representing the area, were all present to greet him. Everybody was at the station as the train pulled in and I was there to give him the ceremonial key to the city.

W got off the train and looked at me, without showing any recognition. I'd gathered all of the Republican office holders from the localities and the legislature standing there to meet him. The very popular and well-known State Senator Bruce McPherson was standing right next to me. But W walked right past me and over to Cathy Hevrdejs, who was an old friend of his from Houston. He gave her a great big hug, a great big kiss, and they were yucking it up together. This, while all the important local politicians were just standing around wondering, "What the hell is going on? What is this? Can we get a hello? Can we get a few words? Maybe a 'great to see you.'" We weren't able to get any of that. Why did we even bother to show up? I felt bad for everyone and for all the time I'd put into bringing together this great reception for the candidate.

For me, it was the last straw with this man. I said, "That's it." He could have just nodded, and that would have been recognition enough. Here, I had introduced him at least ten times. God knows I had a hell of a lot of enthusiasm in the beginning, but now that enthusiasm was evaporating (and it totally disappeared during his time in the White House, by the way).

It must have been a month later that I got a call from Katy Boyd, who was the *grande dame* of Republican politics in the state of California. Katy was the biggest Republican fundraiser there ever was. She has since passed on, but what a woman and what a lady! She knew every president, she knew every vice president. She knew every senator. She just had that charm. She was very into politics and spent a lot of money on politics. What do they say, "Money is the mother's milk of politics?"

Katy called and said, "Denny, darling, oh, have I got good news for you. Our boy Georgie is coming into town. He's flying in just for Thursday night. And he's with his father. His father will be going up to the Bohemian Club, but George W. will be here for dinner Thursday night. And, Denny, we'd like to have you introduce him in your own inimitable fashion. You know how he loves to have you introduce him. It's mostly Lincoln Club people who will be at the dinner—a buffet at my house. Cocktails will be at six o'clock."

I said, "Katy, I'm not able to make it."

"Oh, Denny, what do you mean you can't make it? Darling, it's your responsibility. You are the president of the club. You are the chairman. Of course you have to make it. All the Lincoln Clubbers are looking forward to seeing you.

We are all looking forward to having you there. Oh, Denny, don't tell me you can't make it."

"Katy, I want to tell you something. It's embarrassing. I mean, how hard I have worked for George W. Bush and he's never even acknowledged my presence for the last two years. I'm fed up. I've had it. I'm not going to be there, Katy."

Katy said, "It's your responsibility, Denny, being the Chair of the Lincoln Club. And, frankly, you are very lucky to have the following that you do here at the Club. There are a lot of people coming to hear you make the introduction. You are so amusing and they always get a good laugh."

I said, "Katy, I've lost my sense of humor."

But she continued to persist, calling me the next morning, and then again.

"Oh, Denny, darling, I just thought I would check with you to see if you feel a little bit better about this. I think that, really, it's quite an honor for him to come by to see us on this fly-through."

And I always repeated the same thing. "Katy, I'm sorry."

However, one Thursday morning, I came to realize that Katy was actually quite perturbed with me, so I called her up and finally agreed. "All right. All right. I have got a few commitments. I'm going to be about 15 to 20 minutes late. But for you, Katy, for you and the Lincoln Club, I'm going to make it. And I will try to be witty and funny, but, as usual, W. and I won't even speak to each other. I'm in that mode now where I'm not even saying *hi* to him."

So I got there about 6:15 and walked through the front door. And there on the other side of the room was George W. No sooner had I walked in when he looked up, waving his hand at me, "Denny! Denny! How great to see you! How great to see you!"

Katy was at my right hand, so I turned to her and said, "Oh, my God, Katy, what a setup this is."

"Well, Denny," she said, "he deserved to stand on his

head and say hi to you."

So that was worth a few laughs, I have got to tell you. I got a lot of mileage out of that story. But at the inaugural, it was back to the former W, who didn't even acknowledge me.

Fast forward six months, and Katy was having another dinner party, but this one involved quite a crew of politicians. This was after the inauguration in July, and George, Sr. (father of W.) was there again, on his way to the Bohemian Club. I was sitting at a table with George Drysdale and several of the Lincoln Club members and here came the entourage walking through. George Sr., along with Arnold Schwarzenegger, walked past me, and then the President paused, turned around, and said, "Denny! Denny, is that you?"

I said, "Mr. President, it certainly is. So good to see you."

He said, "We have had some good times together, haven't we? You've certainly worked hard for our party, I'll tell you."

I was thinking that was the nicest thing, that he recognized me, and turned back to say hello. It had been a long time since I'd seen him and he still remembered me.

And no, Katy hadn't put him up to it. Afterwards I asked her, "Katy, did you have George Sr. say hi to me?" Katy replied, "No, I didn't even think about it. I wasn't even sure you were coming."

So it meant a lot to me. It sure did. I just thought George Sr. had a lot of class. My heavens, I really liked that guy.

Where are the Leaders?

When it comes to politics, I've usually thought of myself as a Republican. I have supported plenty of Republican candidates, of course, as I was president of the Lincoln Club of Northern California. But from what I'm seeing today, the Republican Party has lost its way. First, the Tea Party nonsense, these radicals who threatened to shut down the government and refuse to raise the debt ceiling, and Donald Trump, a man whose ethics and morals are completely absent—that's not the Republican Party I was proud to be a part of, whose candidates I worked for. I don't want to have any part of the current crop.

I liked Republicans like Pete Wilson and Tom Campbell. I can't believe that as huge as America and the Republican Party are, that we can't find a hero, another Teddy Roosevelt. I'd take a Harry Truman or a John Kennedy type. Because like all thinking Americans who recognize the trouble we're in, who see the need for true leaders, I put our country ahead of any party.

In the pilot's seat of a Cessna 414 Chancellor

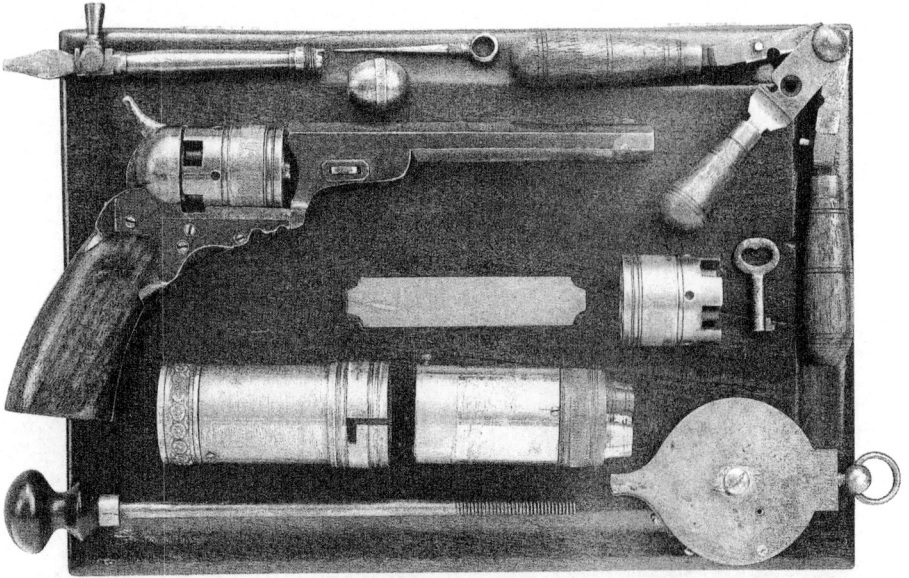

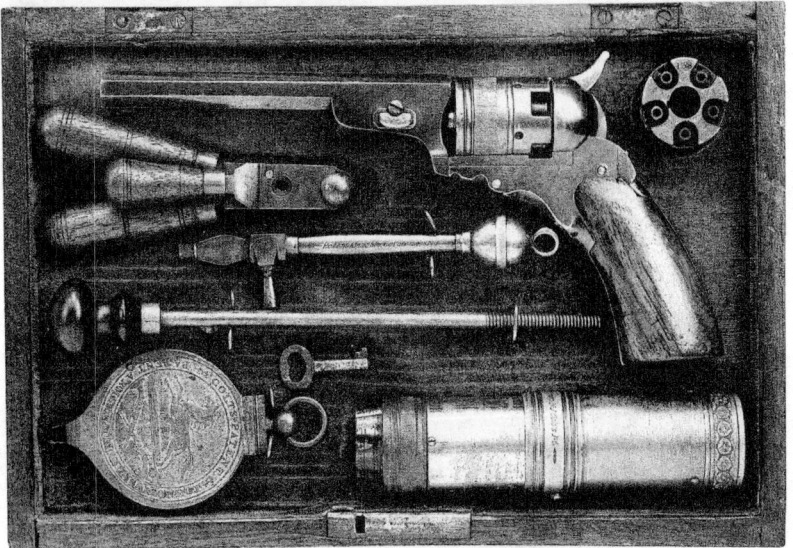

Rare Colt Paterson firearms from Denny's Collection: A Baby Paterson Revolver, Serial # 138, .28 caliber, 5 shots with a 4 1/8-inch barrel; Rare combination of a straight back cylinder and flat butt grip in a mahogany case.

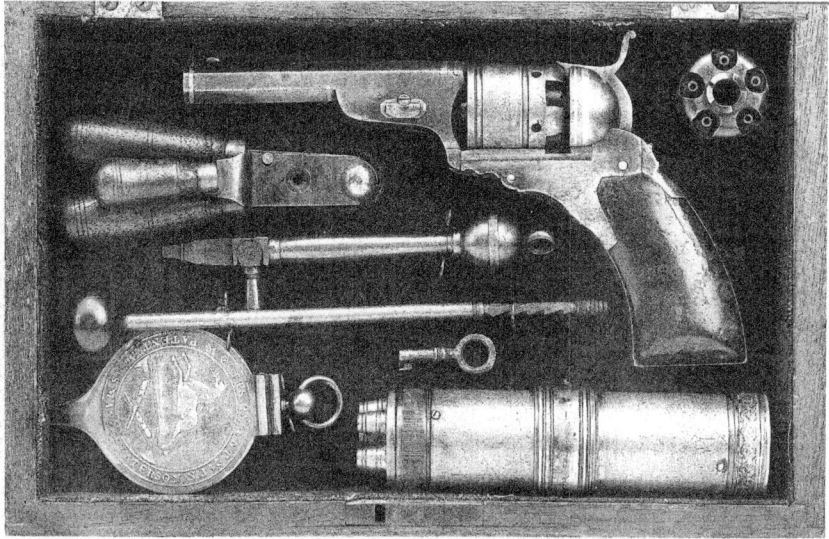

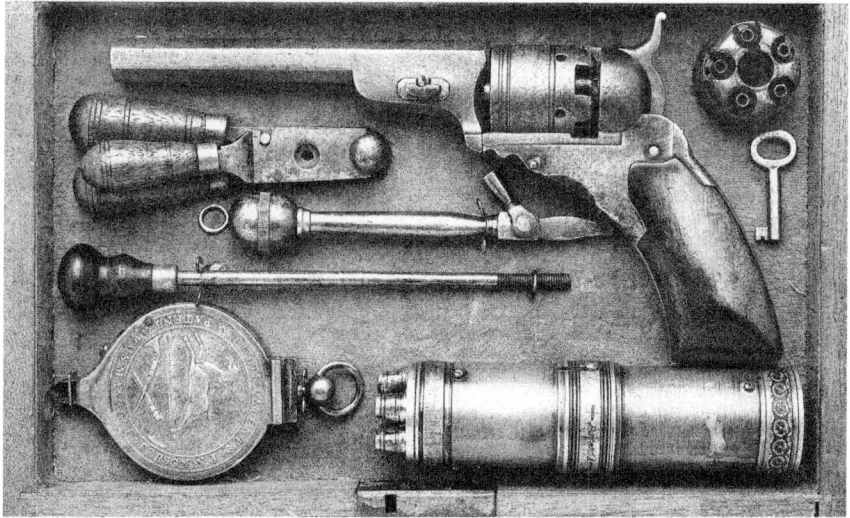

A Baby Paterson Revolver, Serial # 164, .28 caliber, 5 shots, with a 3 1/8-inch barrel. Blued finish; and a Baby Paterson Revolver, Serial # 191, .28 caliber, five shots, with a 4-inch barrel, and a cylinder scene of the centaur pattern. Presented in a varnished walnut case with bevel lid.

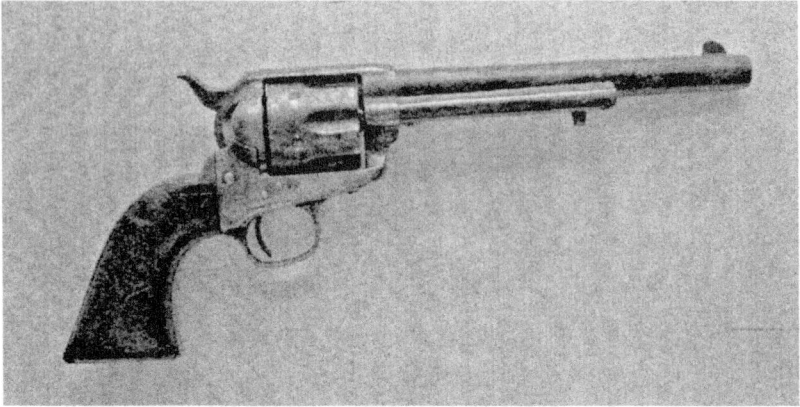

The Colt Army 45 from Custer's Last Stand (1873),
as featured in Denny's dream.

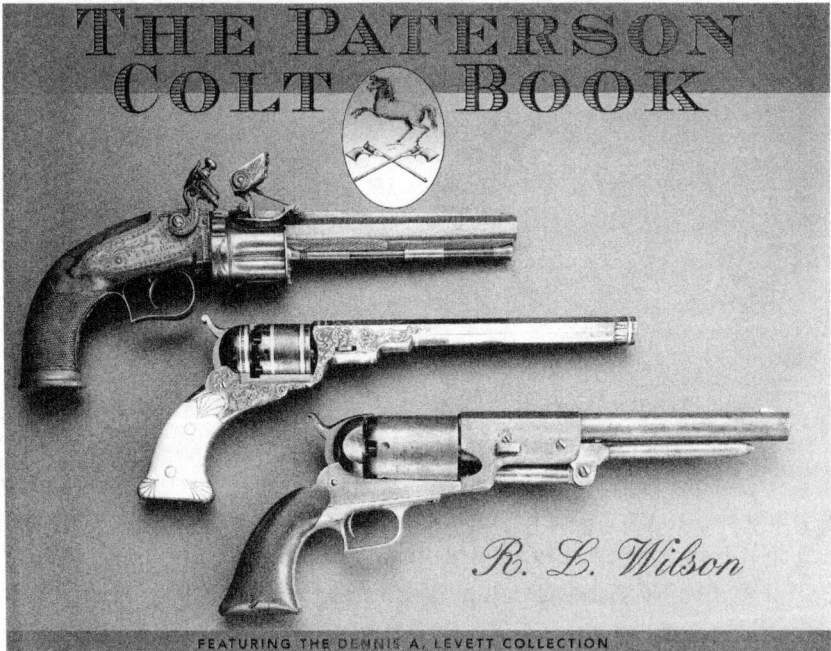

"The Paterson Colt Book: Featuring the Dennis A. LeVett
Collection" by R.L. Wilson and Dennis A. LeVett
was published in 2001.

Jeffrey Richardson, Gamble Curator of Western History, Popular Culture and Firearms (left); Denny LeVett (center); and W. Richard West, Jr., President and CEO of the Autry Museum of the American West, Los Angeles, at the Grand Opening of "The Balance of Power on the American Frontier" exhibit, featuring "The Dennis A. LeVett Collection." Says Denny, of this honor: "I am very proud that my guns are a part of such a significant keeper of our Western history and culture."

Denny, the Gun Collector (2016)

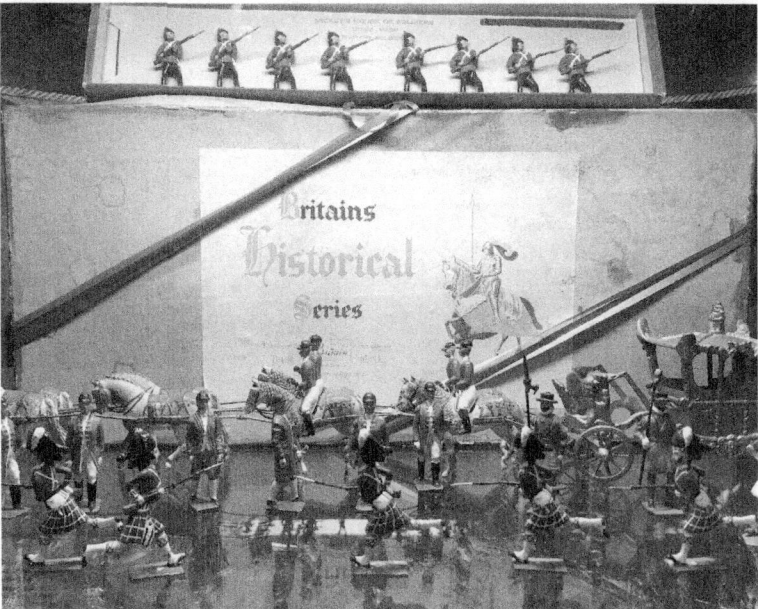
Some of LeVett's highly prized "Britains" toy soldiers

A display case, featuring LeVett's antique collection is on exhibit for all to enjoy at The Cypress Inn, Carmel-by-the-Sea, California

More of LeVett's toy soldiers and antique books

GARAGE STYLE
magazine

The cover story of Garage Style Magazine featured
LeVett's Ferrari Collection in the Summer of 2017

At the wheel

Some of LeVett's classic cars

The Dino Ferrari Coup, Serial # 18, at the Cypress Inn

In 2008, with Rudy Giuliani, former Mayor of New York City

Henry Kissinger and Condoleezza Rice (foreground)
with Denny and Jeanne LeVett at the Lincoln Club (2015)

Former California Governor Arnold Schwarzenegger with
Denny and Katie Boyd at the Fairmont Hotel in San Francisco

John McCain and Denny

A replica of a Cape Dutch-style home he first spotted while traveling in South Africa, LeVett's favorite house he ever built is located on the 17 Mile Drive in Pebble Beach, California.

LeVett's former home in Benbow Valley, on the East Fork of the Eel River in Garberville, was designed by renowned architect Julia Morgan.

Patricia Royce and Carmine Esposito at Carmel Dog Care, a two-acre home away from home for local canines in Carmel. Lucky dogs include Sophie, Desi, Ernest, Brick, Hyden and Strutz (right)

Denny pictured with his favorite Cessna 414 Chancellor and a 1965 Porsche 365 GTB, departing Palo Alto Airport.

The elegant entrance to The Cypress Inn

Old movie posters adorn the walls of The Cypress Inn*

*All likenesses of Doris Day courtesy of the Doris Day Estate

Jeanne, Denny, Hyden II, and Strutz II, at The Cypress Inn, Christmas 2017

Celebrating Doris Day's 92nd Birthday: Jeanne, Doris and Denny*

The Dennis A. LeVett
Cardiovascular Care Center

87
ENCINA

Ribbon Cutting Day, September 29, 2016, at "The Dennis A. LeVett Cardiovascular Care Center" at the Palo Alto Medical Foundation. From left to right: Mara Hook, Casey Crayne, Jeanne LeVett, Kate LeVett Crayne, Dr. Elizabeth Vilardo, Denny LeVett, Dr. Greg Engel, Duncan Lockhart Matteson (foreground), Dr. Ben Mazer, Shirley Matteson, and Dr. Conrad Vial.

Denny with his dear friend
Duncan Lockhart Matteson

Hyden II and Strutz II

LIFE'S MISCELLANY

From Riches to Rags,
A Story of Two Dennys

My daughter, Amanda, had a best girlfriend named Tricia Burns; they were classmates at the Santa Catalina School in Monterey, California. They did almost everything together. On this one warm summer day, I left Carmel and headed up to my main office in Palo Alto. Amanda and Tricia came with me, along with my then-wife, Karen. The two girls were young teenagers at the time.

I was driving the old 1962 Jaguar. This was the 3.8 Sedan. God, I loved that car! It was black with a tan interior and wire wheels. A beautiful car. That's one I wished I would have kept. Classy as all hell! But anyway, we were headed up Highway 17—whatever possessed me to take 17, I don't know. But it was a pretty warm summer day and as I was tooling along through Scotts Valley, I noticed that the water temperature gauge was going up. It occurred to me that we should probably have lunch at the summit where I could let the car cool down a bit. There was a gas station up there where I could check if there was sufficient water in the radiator.

Well, up at the summit on 17 was also a "Denny's" restaurant, a franchise of the multi-million dollar diner chain that has over 1,500 locations in the United States alone. So I said, "Well, girls, I want to see how the re-decorating is going at the restaurant. Let's stop off and have lunch."

As we walked in, I commented to Amanda and Tricia that not one bit of redecorating had been done. It was still the same old brown, yellow, and orange colors. That would have been fine, I said, if it were Autumn, but it wasn't Autumn yet, it was still summer and the colors needed to be something zippy and exciting. I continued my charade by saying that I was going to call the main office *right away* and make this a top priority. They needed to get on this immediately! I didn't care if they were busy in the summertime, I feigned. This was embarrassing!

Amanda must have thought, "Oh gosh, I guess Dad really *does* own Denny's restaurants." Her friend, Tricia, well she was absolutely convinced that I did.

It was about a month or so later when I got a phone call from Bruce Redding, who, along with Jerry Burns (Tricia's father) owned the Rolls-Royce-Jaguar automobile agency in Monterey.

Bruce said, "Hey, Denny how about a glass of wine? Can you make it tonight?"

I said, "Yeah, Bruce, I guess I can, sure."

"Well, good. I'll see you at the Pine Inn about 5:00pm."

"Sounds good to me," I agreed.

So, five o'clock found me at the Pine Inn on Ocean Avenue in downtown Carmel-by-the-Sea with Bruce Redding. Bruce started off the conversation by saying, "Denny, for a man of your stature, a man of your position in life—why are you driving that old, old, old, Jaguar? And why would you drive it if you weren't sure you could make it over the hill or not?"

I realized right away that Tricia had told her father about our climb up Highway 17. Jerry must have suggested to Bruce that he make a pitch to me to buy a new car.

So he continued, "Denny, here you are, you own the Denny's restaurant chain and you own the Vagabonds Inn chain. both very successful enterprises. Don't you think you can afford to own a Rolls-Royce, the finest car in the world? Don't you think a man of your stature should be driving a Rolls-Royce?"

Of course, he had been confused about the hotel thing. I owned the one-of-a-kind, exemplary Vagabond's House Inn in Carmel, where the poet Don Blanding composed the famous poem Carmel-by-the-Sea, not the chain of cheap motels.

But he went on and on. Then finally, he said, "Denny, I want you to come outside with me." We walked out front to Ocean Avenue, where to my astonishment, I find that he has loaded the entire block with a display of Rolls-Royces! There was every type of Rolls-Royce you could think of; from a Rolls-Royce convertible, to a Rolls-Royce two-door Hooper, to the big four-doors.

I didn't laugh and I never gave myself away. I'd kept a straight face throughout all of this silly business. "Bruce, Bruce, I'm going to be really honest with you," I said, "I'm not a Rolls-Royce kinda guy. I'm just not. I think it's the most ostentatious car there could possibly be. Why would I want to drive a Rolls-Royce? Maybe a Bentley, but certainly not a Rolls-Royce." I said it as nicely as I could.

He was unruffled. "Well, Denny," we can take care of you with a Bentley, too. Not to worry. Or the latest Jaguar."

I didn't want to prolong this. "Bruce, let me tell you something . . . I don't own Denny's restaurants. I was just joking with the girls! I don't own that chain. And Vagabonds Inns, that's an East Coast, Florida, Louisiana business; a chain of cheap motels. I don't own that either. If you saw my Vagabond's House Inn, you would never confuse it with the motel chain again."

Well, I did offer to pay for the wine, but Bruce just left shaking his head. He sent all the Rolls-Royces back to the agency and dropped me like a hot potato.

Things with Engines

I know some people turn to flying for no other reason than it's a practical form of transportation. And although it certainly became so for me, to get back and forth from Carmel to Palo Alto, California, and all those trips flying down to Mexico, I loved flying for years before it became a matter of practicality for me. When I was young, practicality was the farthest thing from my mind! It was a thrill. It was the adventure. It was being able to leave the Earth for the skies. Growing up, my heroes were movie pilots—from Dennis Morgan in "God is My Co-Pilot" to John Wayne in "Flying Tigers."

And, oh yeah, it was a really manly thing to be able to fly an airplane. I still feel that way. I like the feel and the look and the idea of flying. It's one thing to drive long distances or drive fast. And you can sail a boat around the world or speed around a lake in one. But flying is magical. You can take off and do what the birds do, what man was never built to do.

Yes, I also have a fascination with classic cars, but no, it doesn't come from having a thing for engines. In fact, it never was that big a deal to me that it was a Chrysler Hemi 300cc engine. Or whether it was a 283 cubic inch Corvette, or whether it was just a plain old Flathead 6. It was the whole design of the car. That's what really was a turn-on.

In Iowa Falls, when I was still just in my late teens, I'd buy a car, smarten it up, and turn it around to resell it. The '55 and '57 Chevy convertibles were really popular. So were the Oldsmobile convertibles. Something that was also hot was the 1950 Ford convertible. The 1949s were kinda hot, too, but the '50s had a little different grill and a different door handle. The '51 and '55 Ford convertibles were also really great cars, but especially the '50 and '51s.

In those days, many people sold their own cars, but some customers came to me because they knew I was honest, and that they could get a good deal. I'd simply put an ad in the paper—"I'm selling my 1957 Oldsmobile Convertible Super 88"—or let people find out by word of mouth. The regular car dealers were asking more money for cars. They needed a higher mark-up than I did because they were running a business. So I sold my cars, got some money, and my grandfather put it into the stock market with shares of ITT. That was cool.

I mean you take some of the greatest designs in the world and they were four cylinder. Everybody loves that Mercedes-Benz 190SL that I've been driving. I could drive it all day every day. Love that car! It's a 4 Banger. It can go 80 miles an hour. I used to commute to the Benbow Inn in that car, from Carmel to Garberville, non-stop; 320 miles and I'd do it in about five hours.

What's the most beautiful design in the world in the latest Ferrari survey? Every National Ferrari Club owner got a questionnaire asking, what's your favorite Ferrari? Not what is your favorite V-12? What's your favorite Ferrari? Well, the Dino Coupe came in No. 1 out of all Ferraris. Does that make me proud to own one? Hell, yes, that car is the sexiest car I've ever seen in my life. When I first saw one I remember thinking, "Oh God! Will I ever have one of these?" The fascination with the Dino Coupe is one of style and beauty, sex appeal, adventure, and of course, the overall performance.

I have to say that my first great car love was a 1950 Ford Convertible. Loved that Ford Convertible! And I finally got one. It took me until college before I had a 1954 convertible. But how about the '55, '56, and '57 Chevy Convertibles? Any one of those was great.

I like some of the new cars, too. I just bought a Fiat Abarth. The company is trying to put Fiat back on the map with this racing car, and I mean it *is* a racing car. It's the fastest little thing I have ever driven in my entire life. So I checked out prices at different Chrysler-Fiat dealers, and they said the Abarth goes out the door for roughly $25,000. But then they've all added $7,000 to the price because each dealership is only getting two. So, I called Sioux Falls and they had just been delivered one 15 minutes earlier. One of my associates got a picture of the car being delivered off the internet and I was able to buy it, without the mark-up.

Today, I am an ardent collector of classic cars—32 of them, in fact; including Mercedes, Porsche, Fiat, Autobianchi, and ten Ferraris . . . all of them red, of course! My garage condo has been featured in Garage Style Magazine numerous times. And every year, I have the honor to bestow the Dennis A. LeVett "Best of Show Award" in the annual Carmel-by-the-Sea "Concours on the Avenue."

The Fiat that was a Ferrari

It was the year of the most famous car designer, Sergio Pininfarina, in the late 1990's at the Concours D'Elegance in Pebble Beach. That Monday following the Concours, Bob Lee, close friend and car collector extraordinaire, invited a group of us to fly in his G-3 to see his unbelievable car collection in Sparks, Nevada. Our group included non-other than Sergio Pininfarina, his wife Georgia, car enthusiast Greg Garrison and his wife Karen, and me.

At lunch, I asked Sergio what his favorite and best design ever was. Without hesitation, he replied, "the Dino Coupe 206 and 246GT." Well, this was the start of a good half-hour chat about our love for the Dino. "I have a Dino Coup," I said, "a red 1968 Transitic 206-246, Serial #18, and I'll be buried in it." Then I asked what my new friend Sergio's next favorite design was. At first, he was hesitant to reply. "I can't discuss it . . . I won't discuss it," he said. It was obvious he was upset. It was only after four long pauses that he finally managed to blurt out: "I'll never speak to Enzo again! It was the Dino Spider Roadster!" Sergio went on, "Enzo Ferrari was so happy with the enormous success of the Dino Coupe that he wanted me to design a Dino Ferrari Spider Roadster. So here I was, commissioned by Ferrari to design *for* Ferrari, built by Ferrari to *be* a Ferrari — and what does he do? He sells it as a Fiat!" Slamming his fist on the table, he yelled, "It's no damn Fiat! It's a damn Ferrari!"

As it turns out, Sergio was absolutely right. The Fiat Dino Spider came about because of Enzo Ferrari's need to ratify a V6 engine for Formula 2 racing, when in 1965, the FIA had set new rules for the upcoming 1967 season. F2 engines were required to have no more than six cylinders, be derived from a road car engine in the GT class, and have at least 500 units produced within a 12-month qualification period. Since at that time, a small manufacturer, like Ferrari, couldn't possibly handle this volume, an agreement was signed with Fiat. The result? The Fiat Dino Spider was born *(Dino was the nickname of Enzo's son Alfredo Ferrari).*

Well, I immediately excused myself from the table and ran to a phone to call a Dr. Cotton in Redondo Beach, who had a red Dino Fiat Spider that I had been thinking of buying. "The timing chain is broken," he said. But that was of no matter to me. Right then and there over the phone, we settled on a price and I bought it on the spot!

Then I casually sauntered back to the table and said, "Sergio, I have a Dino Ferrari Spider, too." He turned and looked me straight in the eye, and said, "The only problem is that they always break a timing chain." This remains one of my favorite car stories about my most favorite driving car. That is, just as long as I don't break a timing chain!

Fernet-Branca

That first trip to Europe, I never had enough money to be anything but a student, and so I fantasized . . . I dreamed that someday I would stay at the Hotel De L'Europe in Amsterdam, a picture of elegance situated where the Amstel River flows into the Rokin Canal. I would meet a beautiful woman there and we would have dinner at the nearby Excelsior, as beautiful a restaurant as I had ever seen.

And now, some twenty years after that first fateful journey, my dreams were coming true. One weekend in 1980, I was to meet a beautiful woman at the Hotel de L'Europe in Amsterdam, the same exquisite hotel on the Amstel River that I had been enchanted with, as a youth.

I had arrived by train from Germany. This was such a milestone for me and I had so looked forward to this moment. Unfortunately, when I arrived at the restaurant for dinner, I was feeling awful, complete with gnarly growlies in the stomach and the cramps of *el producto* like you wouldn't believe. So, there I was sweating in front of this gorgeous woman sitting across the table from me and thinking to myself, "How in the hell am I going to end this? A cyanide capsule?"

I wanted this to be a special evening, and, instead, it was falling flat on its face. My date excused herself. She went to the ladies room, and the waiter came over and said, "You're not feeling well."

"How did you know?"

"I know these things. And with you, you can really tell."

"I'm feeling really awful, absolutely awful. I've got cramps. I can't believe in my stomach."

"Don't worry," he responded, "I will fix you up."

"How many days will it take?"

"I'll fix you up, and in ten minutes, you'll feel like a new man."

The waiter then proceeded to bring over a bottle of *Fernet-Branca* and displaying it to me, said, "You will have a good, generous shot of this and in ten minutes you will feel perfect. Be forewarned, however, it tastes awful, so prepare yourself. You're going to have to drink it straight down."

At this point, I would have done anything, absolutely anything, even make a deal with the Devil—except the Devil didn't have anything to do with it. So I went ahead and scarfed it down. "Oh My God!" It burned and it did taste horrible, but son of a gun, in ten minutes I felt like a new man! I wish to hell I'd had Fernet-Branca that morning before I got there. But anyway, my dinner guest returned and we had a wonderful weekend together.

Humor is the Salve of Life

One of the best laughs I've ever had took place at the Sahara Hotel on the Strip in Las Vegas, where the great comedian, Don Rickles, was a fixture at the Sahara.

I was in Las Vegas with my friend, Arnold Chernoff, for the hottest gun show in the world, hotter than London or Dusseldorf or Belgium. Arnold was a noted gun collector and the son of a very prominent psychiatrist, who had authored a number of very important books in her field. They lived together in a huge mansion in Chicago. And speaking of huge, Arnold was huge. At the time, I think he was 565 pounds. Anyway, Arnold and I and some of our other gun collecting friends were all sitting in the front row of the auditorium at the Sahara, enjoying Don Rickles. Arnold was directly in front of Rickles, sitting across two chairs. He always had to have one chair for one bun, and a second chair for the other one. He was a sight.

Rickles had being doing a routine on what kind of work people did for a living, and at one point, he looked down at Arnold and said, "So little boy, what do you do?"

Arnold replied, in a deep, scratchy, husky voice, "I'm a jockey."

Well, it brought the house down! I mean, I never heard such a big laugh in all my life. I think the laughter went on for 15 minutes. It was priceless.

Medical Miss Practice

I haven't always done well with doctors. Back in 2006, I went to see Dr. Richard Hell for a colonoscopy. *Hell* was an old German name, and he liked being "Dr. Hell." One of his chief competitors was Dr. Doom. Anyway, during the colonoscopy he said to me, "Denny, look at this," while pointing at the screen displaying the scope image. "Look at the size of that polyp. That is a big, big polyp and it's serious. We're gonna have to take that baby out."

Well, three days later, I was on the operating table after two specialists from Northern California came to Carmel to examine me and insisted that the polyp had to come out immediately. When I asked if they knew for sure that it was cancer, I was told, "We *know* it's cancer. It's got to come out right away. We can do it on Saturday." So they had me in surgery three days after finding the polyp, making me believe that I had cancer and that it was very serious.

"I'm supposed to be flying to England to go pheasant shooting at Ben's Pond Estate," I told them. I went last year and the year before and I just can't miss it." They told me there was nothing to the operation, that I'd be fine. That there was very little, if anything, to worry about. I would have the colostomy bag for only about two weeks. Not to worry, they were catching it in plenty of time.

When I awakened from the anesthesia, the first thing I recall was the doctor saying, "You don't have any cancer anymore." He continued to tell me how lucky I was and that I didn't need chemotherapy or radiation.

My intuition was telling me something wasn't quite right, but I pushed any doubts aside and reminded myself that they were the experts. Anyway, I was a quick healer and was home from the hospital in just two weeks. Come

Christmas and New Year's Eve, I was doing just fine. In fact, I even danced up a storm on New Year's Eve.

But the next night I came down with this unbelievable fever; 103 degrees. My friend, Jim Heisinger, rushed me to the hospital. It was obvious that I had developed an infection. This put me in the hospital for two more weeks with all these wires and needles and tubes sticking into and out of me.

When I was finally released from the hospital, the doctors claimed that I had beaten the infection, until only three days later when the fever returned, even worse than before. So back it was to the hospital for another three weeks with a serious staph infection. Later, one nurse, who was present at the time, told me that I almost died. "I shouldn't be telling you this, but we didn't think you were going to make it, Mr. LeVett." (also, she was very pretty and she liked me.)

They wound up giving me a "PICC" (Peripherally Inserted Catheter) for intravenous administration of antibiotics over an extended period of time. A technician came to my house to check it every day. There I was, at home after spending a total of about a month and a half in the hospital, with this machine pumping antibiotics into my heart and blood vessels every 45 minutes. It would take an entire four months, before I was finally able to recover my health.

All these medical problems, for all that time, were for what I was told was cancer, but later, I discovered that it wasn't cancer at all. I had begun to get suspicious again and called over to talk with Dr. Hell. His assistant Rose answered the phone. I told her that I felt like hell. I said, what I've been through feels like a death warrant.

She sounded surprised and asked what I meant about *what I'd been through*. I said, about having cancer. Rose was taken aback. She said, "You didn't have cancer, Denny."

"Really, Rose? I was told that I did. That it had been removed."

She said she would talk to Dr. Hell and get me the pathology report the next day. She was surprised that I hadn't ever seen it.

The following day, I received the report and had it read by a couple of doctors in Palo Alto. They stated very simply that what I had had was a *pre*-cancerous polyp. *Not* cancer. Well, let's face it, everything is pre-cancerous, your thumb, your nose, your whackydo are all pre-cancerous. But bottom-line, I never had cancer.

I went to see my old friend Dr. Carl Bergstrom and put the pathology report on his desk. Now, Carl has been a friend of mine for a long, long time. He saved my life once, literally, a number of years ago when I was bitten by a brown recluse spider. I was unrolling a piece of carpet one Saturday morning when I got this searing pain in my finger. I was feeling faint. The pain was unbelievable. I called out for my wife to call Dr. Bergstrom. He said, "Denny, thank God you found me. Get in here right away." When I arrived at his office, he took a look at my finger and said, "You've been bitten by a brown recluse spider. Without a doubt!" He gave me an antidote shot right away and it saved my life. I don't think I'd be here today if he hadn't known how to treat me.

So when Carl read the report and concurred that I never had cancer, but just a pre-cancerous polyp, I had confidence in his diagnosis. What a relief — and what an ordeal!

LeVett vs. Air China

As anyone who knows me knows, I have a problem making too many commitments, what with my real estate, politics, cars, guns, and writing a book. Anyway, in this situation, I was going on a trip to China, with DiRoNA, the Distinguished Restaurants of North America. It's one of the top restaurant alliances, and I was a past president. The timing was such that right in the middle of this trip, I was supposed to be in Pebble Beach to accept the presidency of the Lincoln Club of Northern California, probably the most prestigious Republican organization in the state, in the West, in the whole country. I was to be sworn in as its president.

However, the DiRoNA trip was a big deal. An awful lot of very notable people from throughout North America were going on this trip to China, set up by the Chinese government. They wanted us there so that they could increase their tourism. This was all good, but as I say, right in the middle of the trip, I was supposed to accept the presidency of the Lincoln Club, as well as emcee the event—something I'd been doing for some twenty-odd years. And that was a big deal. I was always the announcer. I was always the jokester.

I recall that the first part of the trip to China was really important, although now, I can't remember exactly why. We were leaving on Monday and getting into Shanghai the next night. I had a few days in Shanghai, then the group was leaving for Hong Kong. So I set it up where I would fly from Shanghai to San Francisco to Monterey, in time for me to make the seminar at Pebble Beach, accept the presidency and make my speech. Afterwards, I would fly back to San Francisco, get on an Air China flight, and rejoin the group in Hong Kong. It didn't sound stupid to me then. Looking back on it, I can't believe I thought it would work.

Anyway, the scene that Monday, departing San Francisco International Airport on Air China to Shanghai, there were only just so many First Class seats, and Karen, my wife at the time, and I, wanted two of them. I had signed up for First Class because that's a hell of a long flight, San Francisco to Shanghai, with one stop along the way because international law, at the time, said they had to switch pilots. The day before we left, it was announced that the ex-president of DiRoNa, who owned Anthony's Fish Market in Boston, had to have a First Class seat, as well. And guess whose First Class seat he got? Karen's. *Hohoho*. I gave in and said, "Okay, give my seat to my wife." I mean, how would it look if I took the First Class seat and Karen wound up in Business Class? The plane was a 747 and right behind First Class was the stairway that went up past the galley to Business Class. So I signed up for a front row bulkhead Business Class seat, which would make it easier to buzz down and see all my friends, then buzz back up when it was meal time. Fine. However, this was the newer 747 that didn't have the galley stairway. The bulkhead seat had a cutout in front for my legs, but then the top part was almost in my face. Whoever designed those seats didn't know what they were doing. Anyway, I sat down and thought to myself, "Uh-uh. There is no way I'm sitting here." I mean, there wasn't 18 inches of space between the wall and me.

I said to the steward, "This won't do." and was told I would have to speak to Mr. W, who was the manager of Air China in San Francisco.

I walked over to Mr. W, and he said to me, "Oh, sorry. You guys have filled up the airplane, *Di* – whatever you call yourself – *DiNona*, whatever. You have do have a seat assigned for you."

I said, "I'm flying all the way to Shanghai, spending only two days there, then flying back on Air China to San Francisco. The next day, I'm flying out again to Hong Kong, so you're making a lot of money off of me. I can't sit in that seat and I will not sit there."

And so, here I was trying to get the seats straightened out, and all of a sudden, there was an announcement of a mechanical problem with the airplane. There would be a couple of hours wait until the airplane was ready to go. We were ushered into the United Airlines First Class lounge, because Air China shared facilities with United. I found myself in the lounge with Michael Martello, the head of the Chaine des Rotisseurs for our area. The Chaine des Rotisseurs is the oldest wine and food club in the world. It started in 1448, in Paris. So, I said to him, "You know something? This two-hour wait is kind of a standard thing. It often means you don't leave until two days later. I don't like this." I was young and crazy and had money in those days, so we both booked First Class tickets on a United flight to Shanghai. We made our reservations with the understanding that if the Air China plane did leave in two hours, we'd get our money back from United.

In fact, it was exactly two hours, when Air China announced that we were cleared to board again. Michael, by now, knew of my dilemma, and he had a plan. He said, "Tell them you are not going to sit in that seat. No way are you flying in that seat when you had a First Class ticket." And then, he suggested a kicker — which I now began to put into action.

As I boarded the airplane, I saw Mr. W. He said, "Oh, Mr. LeVett. Have you solved your problem, Mr. LeVett?"

I said, "It's up to *you* to solve my problem, Mr. W."

"But I'm afraid we have a big problem, Mr. LeVett, there are no more seats," he responded.

"Mr. W, there are four huge First-Class seats behind Business Class!"

"Oh, that's for the pilot and crew," he answered.

"Don't tell me the whole crew is going to be using them at the same time and you have nobody flying the airplane. I want one of those seats, because I have to get some sleep. I'm flying to Shanghai, but will be turning around and coming right back to San Francisco in only just a few days."

"No way. No you can't," he insisted.

Trying not to smile, I delivered the kicker, "I'm sorry, then please get my bags off the airplane!"

Mr. W was startled. "What? Get the bags off the airplane? No, I can't do that."

"Then give me a good seat, not one where I have got the bulkhead hitting me in the face," I said.

"No. I can't do that."

"I'm sorry, but I'm not going to fly under these conditions. I paid for a First Class seat, and you're trying to jam me in this ridiculously small seat. Get my bags off this plane right now!"

"*Please*," I added with a sarcastic smile.

"What about your wife?" he asked.

"She can stay on," I said.

"I'll have to speak to the pilot," Mr. W said.

I can just imagine what he was saying, in Chinese, of course, "Captain, I have dumb-shit American and he is trying to bluff me. He says he is going to get off the airplane. Tell him that you won't allow it, that he can't have his bags taken off the plane, that you will not allow it."

Mr. W returned. "Mr. LeVett, I spoke to the captain. He says, absolutely no way. I am sorry. He says, tell LeVett he is to sit in the bulkhead seat.'"

I pulled out my United ticket, and said, "Okay, Mr. W, do you see this? It's a ticket leaving for Shanghai in two hours on United Airlines, First Class. I'm flying United."

I paused for a moment to let him think he had won. Then I said, "I want my bags off now. Right now!"

That caught him up short. "No, you can't do that. No way."

I said, "Mr. W, see this? This is my briefcase. I have this and another carry-on bag. I'm going to walk off the airplane right now, and under international law, you cannot take off with my bags. International law says you cannot fly my bags without me."

Mr. W was nearly apoplectic. "Mr. LeVett, you can't do this. You cannot do this."

"Mr. W, I want one of those seats. And if I don't get one, I'm taking the United flight. You can see right here that I have the tickets. And you already know that I'm flying back on Air China to San Francisco on Saturday."

"Oh, LeVett, you can't do this." He picked up the phone and called the pilot. *(Imagine: "Pilot, dumb-shit LeVett, he out-bluff me!")*

"Okay, LeVett, alright. You pulled a trump card on me. You *can* have one of those four seats."

"Thank you, Mr. W, I said politely. I appreciate it. Now, my friend who has that other bulkhead seat, I would also like my friend to come back here and have one of these First Class seats."

That friend was part of DiRoNa, and owned Ernie's in San Francisco. He was as pissed as I was at the situation. So Mr. W went up front and spoke with him. He returned with a perplexed look on his face, and said, "Mr. LeVett, he doesn't want to change seats. He wants to stay where he is sitting. With you not there, he has all the room he needs."

I had to laugh. "Okay, have a good day, Mr. W."

So, there I was, flying to China in this huge, separate cabin, almost all to myself. During the middle of the night, a pilot came back to take a nap, and later, so did a cute stewardess. We got to China. We had a great time. (This funny note, my friend Martello is a big guy, about 350 pounds, who looks like a Buddha. A number of the DiRoNa people would run into Martello, figuratively, and bow and say, "Oh, Buddha. Oh, Buddha." Martello said to me, "The next one that bows to me, I'm going to rip his head off.")

When Saturday afternoon came, I wished everyone goodbye. The flight was to take off at five o'clock. I arrived at Air China with my bags. I had made arrangements to let the other bags go with Karen. My flight took off on time. It was interesting, because in First Class there were only four people, including myself. Not bad. And we were going to

San Francisco. Great. Taking off was a little bumpy, getting up in the sky was not just a little bumpy, it was borderline moderate to severe turbulence, and we were all over the sky. I mean wing tip to wing tip, nose in the air, nose down. So, there I was trying to write my speech, and the stewardess (I think we still called them that then) offered me a drink. I said, "No, thank you. I've got to write my speech." But then, after working on my speech for 15 minutes, my writing was all over the page from the air turbulence. It looked like I just failed a lie detector test. The stewardess was gorgeous. I said, "Excuse me. I would love to have some vodka."

"Vodka?" she responded, with raised eyebrows.

"Yeah, vodka."

"Oh, so sorry," she said. "We don't have vodka."

"On a flight like this and you don't have vodka?"

"We don't have vodka," she said, "We have Great Wall China wine. We have other great bamboo wine. We have Jack Daniels."

"I just don't feel like Jack Daniels right now," I said.

"We have brandy. You can have brandy. We give you Courvoisier now?" she offered.

I said, "It's only 5:15 in the afternoon, I'm just not in the mood for Courvoisier."

But, after thinking about if, I decided I would give her one more try. I went back to the galley to see if she had anything else I could drink. At that point, I would even drink gin. The turbulence was still heavy, and, of course, the seat belt signs were on, but no one cared. China Air, at least at that time, a sign was only just a sign. As I was holding onto the wall and the ceiling, one of the cupboard doors in the galley flew open and was swinging back and forth. Then, another flew open and inside I saw that there were about five different types of vodka on the shelf. I pointed to them and said to the stewardess, "Vodka!"

She said, "Ohhh, you mean vodka."

I said, "Yes, that is what I mean."

"My fault. I'm sorry," she said. "There are so many

dialects in Chinese. I used one of the dialects that wasn't familiar to you. Yes, vodka."

I went back to my seat and she brought me a tumbler of vodka neat. No ice, no citrus. I smiled at her and said, "Okay. Thank you. May I have some ice?"

She said, "Ice?"

I said, "Yes, please, could I have some ice?"

And she said, "Ice?"

"Oh, you think I'm saying 'eyes.' No, *ice*."

"Ice?"

Then, this really handsome Chinese man who was sitting bulkhead seat in First Class, said in beautiful English, "Excuse me. He means *ice*."

"Oh, ice! Of course," she said, and was back in only a moment with the ice.

Now, at this point I'm thinking, this is stupid. I wasn't going to be able to drink this. The plane was jumping all over the sky. There must have been a couple of Mig 21 pilots in the cockpit testing the structural limits of a 747. They were putting it through twist and turn. They weren't even slowing down for this turbulence.

The nice gentleman and I chatted for a bit. "You're returning home?" he asked.

I said, "Yes. I'm being inducted as president of the Lincoln Club of Northern California."

In beautiful English, he said "I'm involved in politics too, and I'm also on my way back. It's great that we will pick up a day. I'm on my way to see the Secretary of the Treasury, Alan Greenspan. Greenspan is a wonderful friend of mine. He has been a great help to me. We have American dollars coming in, and we want all the American dollars we can get. Greenspan really helps me with how to run the Federal Reserve."

I said, "Oh, are you with the China Federal Reserve?"

He said, "Yes, I'm the head of the Chinese Federal Reserve."

"I'll be darned. Congratulations," I said. Pretty soon we

got to the cruising altitude. It got much calmer. He and I had dinner together and yucked it up a bit. It was a pretty nice flight actually. We wound up landing in San Francisco a little bit late because of the early turbulence being so bad. By that time, my new friend called me Dennis. He said, "Dennis, tell you what. They will let me disembark first. Don't worry about the seat belt signs. Let's get up and go to the back. They will open this door first so I can get out and get a cart. (He used the word jitney.) You mentioned you had a plane waiting for you. Why don't you come along with me and I'll give you a ride. We'll get through customs faster."

I said, "I would love it. Thank you very much."

The doors of the aircraft opened, and there I was with the head of the Federal Reserve of China—and who was standing right there in front of me? None other than Mr. W! Startled by the sight of us, he looked up at me and said, "LeVett! LeVett! It's you, LeVett!"

I said, "Well, Mr. W, what a pleasure to see you again. Oh, and your lovely assistant is here with you. Nice to see you again, too."

"Hello, Mr. LeVett," she said, smiling back.

"Well, *toodle-oo*, Mr. W," I said. "I'll see you again tomorrow afternoon." That's because *today*, he was at the gate to greet the arriving VIPs, but *tomorrow* he would be on my flight going back to China.

That night, thanks in part to Mr. W, I gave one of the funniest acceptance speeches I ever made. It brought the house down! The next day, I was back in San Francisco for the flight on Air China to Hong Kong. And once more, there was Mr. W.

"Hello, again," I said, with the widest grin.

"LeVett! So good to see you, Mr. LeVett."

And oh, did they take good care of me going back!

TSA Over the Top

There is no person of a sound mind who doesn't want to feel safe. Especially when we board an airplane that will soon be flying six miles above the Earth. We all think it's a good idea that our fellow passengers not have bombs and firearms when they fly. That said, we have given a little too much authority to the TSA.

For instance, there are limits on how much toothpaste we can carry in our ditty bag. We can't bring a bottle of water through the TSA checkpoint. And there's that great *kerfuffle* about carrying a tiny-bladed knife with us; one of those tiny Swiss army knives with a blade that's less than an inch and a half long and not nearly as dangerous (sturdy) as a Cross ballpoint pen.

It's easy to become annoyed with the ridiculous pettiness of the mindless rules, and impossible not to get angry with the TSA employees who are likely worried that any complaining passenger pleading reason — someone who is obviously not a terrorist — is possibly a management spy. They worry that showing some common sense could cost them their job.

When having to deal with most government authorities, you don't really know when you are going to run up against people who were attracted to the job simply because of the gun, the uniform, and the badge. In a regular job, they would be the types who wimp out and don't stand up for their own rights. Now with the arbitrary authority of their employment, they can push other people around.

My wife, Jeanne Cox LeVett and I, both highly seasoned international travelers, have long known the benefits of patience while traveling. Jeanne and I ran up against just such TSA arbitrariness at five o'clock one morning as we were making our way back home to California, starting at the Albany, New York airport. We were there in Albany, NY, visiting Jeanne's sister, Robin Esposito, brother-in-law, Michael Esposito, and Michael's cousin, George Nickolettas, who couldn't wait to come visit us in Pebble Beach to play a few rounds of golf at Pebble Beach, Spy Glass, and Spanish Bay. But I digress . . . Jeanne was the first victim. The TSA scanner picked up two unidentifiable objects in her carry-on luggage. They were two small antique Steuben crystal glass bowls that became apparent when her bag was opened for inspection.

That should have settled the matter, but it didn't. The TSA rubbed the glass, as well as the inside of her bag with those treated cloth pads designed to find traces of explosives. Need it be said? They tested negative. Then the officers insisted on putting the bowls through on the conveyor belt, thinking, perhaps, that some sort of explosive device might be hidden in the crystal glass. It didn't seem to matter that this exercise in speciousness was holding up hundreds of passengers waiting to go through Security. It no doubt added to the frustration of those waiting to get to their planes that the TSA showed no sense of urgency whatsoever. Of course, the officials themselves were not in danger of missing a flight.

Then, while Jeanne was repacking her bag, my luggage caught the attention of the TSA security guards, sowing concerns that brought TSA supervisors and sheriff's deputies on the run. One official, a short man, ran around the security area yelling, "Shut it all down!" meaning the screening machines, and "Cordon off the area!" I found it hard to believe that all this craziness was going on since I knew there was nothing the least bit threatening, let alone dangerous in my bags. (The little TSA Chief reminded me of the Charlie Chaplin character in "The Great Dictator.")

All four lines of people with their carry-ons were stopped. The martinet and his marionettes stood peering at the luggage monitor screen. I invited them to go ahead and open up my bag to see for themselves. It took them probably fifteen minutes to finally decide to take me up on my offer, at which point the truth was revealed.

As many people who visit the Vagabond's House Inn and the Cypress Inn in Carmel know, I am an internationally renowned collector of antique toy soldiers, and in my bag were three of them; one lead and two of cast iron. Not only were these obviously just toy soldiers, but they were only about three inches high.

Also, if you don't know, I am not someone who could be mistaken for The Hulk. First, because I'm a bunch of inches under six feet, and second, because I am one of the most dapper dressers you might ever hope to meet. I was wearing a glorious brown suit with a pink shirt, pink tie, pink socks, and pink handkerchief in my breast pocket. Mere words don't do my appearance justice. And Jeanne, as ever, was the picture of appealing dignity. Only the sartorially challenged would view us as a potential threat.

The TSA people emptied everything out of my bags into luggage bins and examined it all carefully. They even opened my two nail clippers, pulling out the nail file, as though something might have been hidden underneath it. When they finished, the man in charge, frustrated that they hadn't found anything, had his minions empty out the luggage bins onto the conveyor belt so that it all could be screened again.

Of course they found nothing. They began putting my things in my bags, not nearly as carefully as they should have, even breaking two small antique model airplanes— one wooden and one plastic, from the 1930s, which I had carefully packed to protect them on the flight.

Jeanne reminded me how lucky I was that I hadn't packed my gun. In fact, I had asked Robin, at the last moment before we left her house that morning, to mail it to me; that I didn't want to bring it on the plane. Was the gun a Glock 10 or an S&W .357 magnum? No, it was a 1938 antique model of an anti-aircraft gun that was also only about three inches high, and hollow inside with no gun bore. The toy soldiers were also from that time period. The detail on them was special. These were valuable antiques.

The whole situation was bizarre. And Jeanne noted that it was miraculous that I, not noted for my patience in the face of idiocy, was able to restrain myself. Asked how this was possible, I said my recent marriage seemed to have imbued me with a greater degree of common sense. And I recognized that had I dealt with the officials from my gut, I probably would have spent a night in the Albany jail. We acknowledged, with appreciation, that two deputies came over after the situation was defused to offer their apologies.

Yes, we want security on our airlines, but does anyone really feel safer in the air today because of how we have been handled over the past fifteen years? That's a significant question, especially considering that virtually a quarter of the guns and knives and other banned items in carry-on luggage make it through the TSA screening process. Ultimately, it's the people who wear the uniforms who provide the best security, and the better hires the TSA makes, and the more common sense that they are allowed to apply to the unique and human situations that come before them, the better it will be for all of us.

Hyden

Have you seen the bumper sticker "Wife and Dog Missing. Reward for Dog?" Well, that's how I felt about my dogs. No offense to my darling wife of today.

Hyden came into my life in 1991. I found him through Dr. Grace Blair, a neurosurgeon who also happened to be the President of the California Poodle Association who raised thoroughbred poodles. I called Dr. Blair and told her, "I want a big, white, male standard poodle."

"I've got one," she said. He's just a baby, and he's already quite large. A little lethargic, but awfully sweet. The price is $1,000. I'll send you photos of him, as well as of the mother and father. He'll be very big and very handsome."

So my wife and I and our daughters, all drove up to Placerville to pick up the poodle. I was so delighted to bring him home. He was the handsomest guy I'd ever seen. And, my God, a little lethargic, as Dr. Blair had implied? I don't think so. Whatever was she thinking? This was the most fun-loving dog I had ever seen. He was jumping up and down all over the place. And he was just so smart, you couldn't believe it. In no time, it was as though English was his first language, instead of "woof". He understood everything I said to him. I could go on and on about this dog, so I will.

Hyden (who I named after the Austrian composer Joseph Hayden, but obviously didn't know how to spell!) would sit with his paws on top of the table. I'd then put my hand down next to his paw. He'd put his paw on top of my hand, and then I'd bring my other hand out from underneath his, and put it back on top of his. Then he'd put both paws on top of my hand. We played this game all the time, from when he was just a little puppy.

Baby Kate would take a stick and poke at Hyden until

he growled. She'd torment him in the rear end and in the eye and in the mouth. Kate loved poking him with a stick. But all he would do is growl and take it. Hyden was kind to Kate and Amanda. Anybody else, he would have taken their arm off because he was a fighter. He'd sneak out and go down to the beach and almost every day come back with blood on his white coat. He was a fighter like no dog I'd ever seen.

Anyway, we'd tell Kate, "Don't, Kate! Do not poke him with the stick. No!" But she was too young to listen. She thought it was the most fun.

One night, right hand to God, we were getting ready for bed and when we pulled the covers back, there, under the covers, was the stick — the one Kate had used to poke Hyden with — and it had been chewed to splinters! Somehow, he had brought the stick with him under the covers and chewed it to pieces. (Shades of *The Godfather* with the horse head, only this wasn't a warning, it was a statement.)

*   *   *   *   *

When Hyden was about 2½, we decided that he needed a friend and that it had to be another big poodle, but this one black. So I found a huge black poodle and named him Strutz, which was my grandfather's surname. Strutz loved children and was the most gentle dog. Hyden did not like Strutz. Strutz would come near him and Hyden would growl. However, Strutz didn't take "grrrr" for an answer. He just followed Hyden everywhere.

Then one night — "It was a rainy night on the west coast of Scotland" — and it was also a rainy night on the west coast of Pebble Beach, Hyden took Strutz out. Word has it that Hyden was seen at the Beach Club, where people were having a late-night party. I got a phone call from someone who saw him through a window. At about eleven o'clock, Hyden arrived home, but there was no Strutz. Not until the next morning around 8:30, when Strutz was heard scratching at the door. We had to look twice to see that it was our

Strutz because he was covered with sand. We speculated that Hyden had pushed Strutz off the cliff down by the golf course holes number eight and nine. Unbelievable. Our suspicions deepened when for two days, Strutz just huddled on the purple leather couch in the family room and didn't move. He had been scared to death.

Of course, as time went on, they acted like brothers. Hyden would go out and Strutz would follow him. Though, when they walked along the top of the cliff, Strutz would kinda veer away from the edge a bit. Then they would go past the Beach Club, stopping by the back door to see if they might beg something to eat. Next they'd walk over to The Lodge, climb the back stairs to the living room and stroll through the lobby and out the front door—like they owned the place. Then they would walk down Palmero past the Spa. Right down the middle of the street, with Hyden in front and Strutz behind him by about four feet. Every time cars would come by, Hyden would wait until the last minute before jumping to the side, leaving Strutz in the middle of the road.

*   *   *   *   *

Everybody talked about Strutz and Hyden. There was no question that I had the smartest big poodles there ever were. One morning, I was driving to the Cypress Inn with the dogs in the back seat; they loved the Cypress Inn. We were on San Antonio, approaching Ocean Boulevard with the classical station KBACH on the radio. The announcer was talking about the composer Haydn. Suddenly, Hyden stuck his head between the seats and peered at the radio. And every time the announcer said the composer's name, Hyden would tilt his head toward me and give me a strange look. This happened maybe a half-dozen times; he looked back and forth, from the radio to me, then back to the radio. I've had lots of dogs, and I've seen lots of dogs—I love dogs—but Hyden was the smartest guy of my life.

Hyden would run up to the front door of the Cypress (he'd been going there for twelve years). Normally, he would go right to the office door that led behind the front desk and push it open. Unless it was locked or closed, in which case he would push at it until I opened it for him. He would then go behind the desk, sit down, and look regal. If I was at the hotel for two hours, he'd be at the front desk the whole time. Sometimes I'd leave him there all afternoon. He loved it. People would walk in and everybody would speak to him. This was *his* hotel.

Every once in a while he would give a "grrrr" to another dog. One time I had Hyden on a leash when we walked in the door and he spied a Great Dane. More than three feet high, the Great Dane was just standing peacefully in the lobby. Hyden walked up to the larger dog, whose owner's eyes suddenly grew to the size of saucers. "Oh, no!" she said.

I couldn't see Hyden's face so I didn't notice that he was bearing his teeth. Hyden had a huge mouth. I mean, like a crocodile. And he was angling for the Great Dane's neck. Luckily, I pulled his leash tight just at the last minute, so there was no attack.

*   *   *   *   *

Hyden was a scamp, oh my God. We lived on the golf course, and Hyden would watch through the window, his tail wagging, as the groundskeepers worked on the fairways and the greens. He would wait, and as soon as the groundskeepers started to drive away, he'd dash out the door and bound into the air, as though on springs, onto the sand traps. Suddenly, you would see sand going up all over the place. It got to a point where he would do a couple of sand traps in a row, not just the twelfth green where we lived, but he'd go down to the eleventh. Sand traps were his thing. It got to a point where the groundskeepers would get really irritated. Understandably. They would see me and they'd come over and ask, "Is that dog around? Keep that dog away from our sand traps. Keep that big white one away from our sand traps."

I'd shrug my shoulders as though there was nothing I could do, and maybe slip them a little something for their troubles, because Hyden just loved playing in those sand traps. He was such a rascal. He liked it best when they had just been raked.

He was fearless, and not just as a fighter. He would leap off the second-story patio at our Rock Lane house; just leap into the air. He was the most graceful dog you ever saw in your life. I came home one afternoon, and when I walked out on the patio, all of a sudden I saw Hyden impaled in the shrubs. All four legs were splayed down into the shrubs. And he looked at me like, "Okay, stupid, get me out of this."

*　　*　　*　　*　　*

One day, a young fellow who was working for me was in my Jeep Grand Cherokee with the dogs in the car. I was driving behind him. He stopped to make a U-turn because he had forgotten something and a car hit him, smashing into the side of the Jeep. The driver was all right, but I was worried about the dogs and took them to the animal emergency room where they checked them over. The dogs hadn't been hurt in the accident, but in the course of examining them, the vet informed me that Hyden had Lymphoma and that the treatment for Lymphoma would normally be Prednisone and acupuncture. Immediately thereafter, as I was on a scheduled trip to New York, I instructed one of my employees to rush Hyden up to Doris Day's favorite veterinarian, a Dr. S., who was a cancer specialist. *Anything* to save my Hyden! I wanted his expert opinion and to know how everything was going with Hyden's health. However, I specifically cautioned him that Hyden should *not* have any chemotherapy treatments. I had been warned that he shouldn't have chemo because of the

Prednisone.

Back in New York, I retrieved a voice mail. It said, "Mr. LeVett, this is Dr. S. I've just started your dog on chemotherapy, and I think we can keep him going for two years."

I phoned him back right away and I said, "No, you can't give him chemo! I told you that. You can't give him chemo!"

About a week later, my employee was driving Hyden back to Pebble Beach from Palo Alto, and stopped off at Dr. S's for a follow-up examination. I thought all was well, but when I returned from New York, I was shocked to learn that the doctor had continued to give Hyden chemotherapy, against my instructions, once again! I called Dr. S and shouted, "You son of a bitch. He should never have had chemo. He should never have it again. He can die."

Dr. S responded, "He'll last a couple more years with this. He'll be fine. I promise you that."

I woke up in the middle of the night and heard a moaning. I went into the living room. There was Hyden, having had horrible diarrhea and throwing up. I opened the door to let him out. He was so weak. He went to the back yard down off the deck.

I called Dr. S on the Thursday of Memorial Day weekend to report on Hyden's ailments. I'll never forget what he said, "Bring him right back. We'll take care of him. Don't worry. Bring him right back. He'll be as good as new."

So I took Hyden up there, thinking, for sure, I could now trust him to take proper care. My driver was behind the wheel and I was in the passenger seat. Hyden put his head between the two seats and looked at me; just stared at me. Then he put out his paw and tugged at my arm. He was saying, "I'll be fine. Don't take me up there. I'll be fine. Don't take me up there."

I wish I had listened to him, but at the time I thought I was doing the best thing. Like so many people, I give more credit than is due to doctors who wear those white lab coats. It gives them an aura of authority. It's why the service manager at a car dealership in San Francisco used to wear a white lab coat—fewer questions and higher bills.

When we arrived at Dr. S's office, they made me wait almost two hours. There was this horrible receptionist who would take a call and then say, "We're awfully busy. I have to put you on hold." She put people on hold, but I could see that there were no other phone calls. She was just making them wait.

As I found out later, Dr. S wasn't even there. He had left for the Memorial Day weekend. But there were other vets present, so I spoke to one of them, a rather nice young man, and I said, "You save my dog's life and there will be a $3,000 tip for you. Just save my dog's life."

"Mr. LeVett," he said, "I don't think you have anything to worry about. We'll save him."

Well, Hyden was there Thursday, Friday, Saturday, and Sunday. And I kept going up to visit him, and every time I had to wait. I couldn't just go in and see him. They had him in a cage. Here was this 85-pound poodle—a big dog—in a cage. Hyden wouldn't even look at me. He turned away. I mean, Jesus!

Anyway, the vet said, "He's going to be fine. He's going to be fine." Then, on Memorial Day night, Sunday night, around midnight, I got a call. "Mr. LeVett, he's dying, he's dying. We need to have you come up right away."

I was in shock. "I can't believe it. Don't let anything happen to him before I get there. I need to be with him."

It was 1:00 a.m. by the time I got there. I walked in to, "Oh, Mr. LeVett, this has been a miracle, an absolute miracle. All of a sudden he's just so much better. We've got to have Dr. S take a look at him in the morning, but I think you'll be able to take him home tomorrow afternoon. Oh, Mr. LeVett, by the way, you owe $4,400 for his care so far."

In shock, I said, "I've already paid twice for chemo at $850 a shot. What else could I owe?"

"Well . . . keeping him here, medications, and caring for him for so many days. That will be $4,400, sir. I can take your credit card now." I threw my credit card down, remarking that "this smells, this really smells."

I spent some time with Hyden, a couple of hours. And my heart was broken. I said to the vet, "You just be sure he's all right. I'll be back to pick him up in the morning." But by then, they said, "Unfortunately, you can't pick Hyden up. You'll be able to pick him up on Wednesday morning. No problem picking him up Wednesday morning. We just have a few final things to do. He will be fine. What a turnaround."

There was one vet that was awfully nice to me, otherwise, the rest were horrible. She kept saying, "He's going to be all right. He's going to be all right."

But the next morning, I got a call saying, "Your dog has died."

"What?!" I shouted. "I'll be right there."

"No. You can't. You can't come up. You can't come up. We don't want you here."

"Why?" I demanded.

"I think they're afraid of you."

I felt like saying "They should be," but I bit my tongue and got into the car.

I went up and got my dog. Nobody there wanted to talk to me or even face me. Dr. S would not return my phone calls. I was tempted to hire a private detective to check into his background. As it was, I filed complaints with the State of California. I sued him. I wrote articles. Every Christmas, without fail, I publish a tribute to Hyden in the *Carmel Pine Cone*. I told everyone about the veterinarian in Aptos, who, in my opinion, had killed Hyden. Doris (Day) never went there again.

But to this day, ten years later, I wake every morning—every morning of my life—around five, and I think of Hyden and how I was responsible. I have shed more tears over my friend, feeling responsible for his death, than anyone can imagine.

*   *   *   *   *

I wanted to take Dr. S to court, but reason prevailed. Reason, not justice. What judge would hold a vet responsible for the death of a patient? I realized that all I could do would be to tell my own story and then let my anger go.

Now, I've finally made a decision that I can't live with this wrenching pain any longer. It probably seems like an obsession to some people, but Hyden and I were so close. I remember, so vividly how he put his hand on my arm. When I've thought about death, it comes to mind that, "Well, Denny, the one good thing about leaving this life is that I'll be with Hyden again."

I've realized, though, that, "I've got to not think about this. This could ruin my life if I keep thinking about it." But in truth, and I can't explain it, nothing has affected me more, and I've certainly had a lot of deaths in my family. But nothing was more precious to me in the world than Hyden. I could carry on a conversation with him and he understood every word I was saying, and I understood him. But enough, it's time to lay him to rest, once and for all. With love.

So I've decided to get two little bronze statues of Strutz and Hyden and put them in the Cypress Inn, which they loved. That was their home.

Strutz

Strutz, my giant Poodle, loved greeting both canines and humans at his home away from home, The Cypress Inn. At the tender age of six weeks, behind the desk at The Cypress, he began to develop his skills as Ambassador to Carmel and as a gentleman. The name "Strutz" was my mother's maiden name, and when searching for a name for my business, it occurred to me that a better combination could not be had. So, I chose "Strutz-LeVett."

One day, I received a call from a local title company officer, Michele. She said, "We have received a bill for an additional $1,800 in termite work."

I responded, "Wait, I didn't authorize that."

Michele then replied, "They couldn't reach you, but they called your partner Strutz, and got the OK."

I said, "Partner Strutz is lying in front of the fireplace shaking his head NO!"

This is but a small example of the many ways both Strutz, and his brother Hyden, touched and shared our lives daily. I wish I could adequately express to you the amount of love and joy both of these boys brought to my family. Sharing space and time with these two magnificent creatures has been without any doubt, one of the greatest experiences of our lives.

Strutz, my brave and stoic boy, died in my arms at 1:30am on Thursday, December 13th, 2007. He had the very best care thanks to Dr. Amanda Sharp, Dr. Karen Fenstermaker, and Technician Greta Stearman of Ocean View Veterinary Hospital in Pacific Grove; Dr. Darren Hawks, Dr. Katja Herrman of Monterey Veterinary Emergency and Specialty Center, and Dr. Colleen Brady of Pacific Veterinary Specialists and Emergency Services. I love you all for the care, compassion and professional expertise you gave to Strutz. Nothing was overlooked and every possible measure was taken in order to keep him pain free, comfortable, and able to maintain good quality of life until the very end. I cannot express how relieved I am to have allowed him to leave us on his own terms, when he was ready. I could not have done this without your constant and unwavering support.

The doctors at Ocean View, Pacific Veterinary and Monterey Veterinary Emergency have given me some hope of possibly restoring my faith in Veterinary Medicine and those who practice it. They have done so much more for my family than they could possibly know. What they have given Strutz and I could not stand in greater contrast to the tragic experience I had with the clinic in Santa Cruz County that resulted in the death of Hyden, while in their care.

To my dear, sweet boys—you remain always in my thoughts and bring me joy, daily. Whether it is a vision of the two of you playing in the surf, running like the wind, or in the custody of our local CHP for speeding through Pebble Beach, it brings a smile to my face and warmth to my heart. May the angels watch over you, now and always.

Afterword

If a scientific expert told me that the weather we had this last year was due to global warming, caused in part by man—and he truly was an expert—I'd believe him. And I wouldn't be surprised because I've never seen anything like this in my lifetime. Not here on the Central Coast of California, in Iowa, where I've been every year of my lifetime, nor in so many different places across this country and around the world. I've been a lot of places. Things have changed.

To be clear, I'm certainly not a liberal. My politics are very tailored around the facts. I am not agenda-driven. I don't vote the party line just because I'm a registered Republican, nor do I just accept other people's opinions. I do my own thinking.

It's funny how in this book, after all these years, I'm speaking about things that have truly shaped my life—like my interest in guns, travel and seeing the world, flying, getting involved in politics, becoming a businessman, and how my interest in beautiful places of the world were born in the magazines of my youth, like *National Geographic, Holiday, Life, Look, Post,* et cetera. They opened my eyes to this amazing planet and produced goals to be achieved. I wanted to be an adventurer, and certainly that was an important part of my life.

But in writing this book, I have been re-awakened to how different life was back in the late '40s through the '50s, and even into the '60s. My God! What a good America we had! In the '60s, it was obviously a different time for me, but I had a sense then that everything was possible. And now, sadly, nothing seems possible.

That's the difference for me. You can't even impart it to the young people today, what it was like back in the middle of the 20th Century. How when you drove downtown in the summer, you left the windows open in the car. How there was a sense of community and trust. That's hard to imagine today, in a world where madmen with guns shoot up schools and churches and movie theaters.

In the northwest part of Iowa, where I'm from, a century before I arrived, the people there were great hunters and fishermen. My God, they lived responsibly, with a deep spiritual sense of being, at one with the earth.

I don't know whether it was a combination of church and state, and the fact we were all brought up working. I worked from the time I was eight or nine years old. I think back on how lucky I was.

When I first began thinking about writing this book, I didn't give a thought to this stuff. But last summer, when I was at Lake Okoboji, my wife Jeanne turned me on to a certain awareness, and that is, what a paradise it was at the time I grew up. Back then, you could be anybody you wanted to be. Really, you could be poor and figure out a way to never be poor again. Lately, I've been having a lot of conversation with people who have the same feeling I do about the greatest time in the world to grow up. For me, it was the 50s and 60s! When I look back on the '60s and the early '70s, I remember scoffing at the hippy thing, but know that they were absolutely right about the Vietnam War.

A lot of what's in this book is about the America that was the shining city on the hill. I want that back. How do we get it back?

-*Denny LeVett*

Awards and Honors

Denny LeVett has been the recipient of numerous awards and honors over the years. He has also served as Chairman, Trustee, and member of many distinguished boards and councils. His generous donations to museums, charities, and civic causes are renowned in his community.

■ The "Dennis A. LeVett Cardiovascular Care Center," in Palo Alto, California, was unveiled in 2016, as a result of his generous donation to the Palo Alto Medical Center.

■ The Autry Museum of the American West, in Los Angeles, California, houses a permanent installation of "The Dennis A. LeVett Collection" of Colt Paterson firearms, first featured in an exhibition entitled "The Balance of Power on the American Frontier."

■ The Cody Firearms Museum, Buffalo Bill Center of the West, in Cody, Wyoming, is the beneficiary of a rare 1836 Texas Model 12" Colt Paterson firearm, on display with a recognition plaque inscribed "as gifted by Dennis A. LeVett."

■ Presenter and namesake of the Dennis A. LeVett 'Best of Show' Award for Carmel-by-the-Sea, "Concours on the Avenue" annual competition.

■ President of The Lincoln Club of Northern California

■ President and Member of Board of Directors, Stanford Financial Co

■ Board of Trustees, Monterey Institute of International Studies

■ Member, Monterey County Sheriff's Advisory Board

■ Board of Trustees, Mid-Peninsula Bank of Palo Alto

■ Member, Carmel Innkeepers Association

■ President, Strutz-LeVett Investment Holding

■ Member, Wilson Council of the Woodrow Wilson Center

■ President of the Distinguished Restaurants of North America

■ Board Member and investor, Greater Bay Bank, Palo Alto, CA

■ Recipient of the 2017 "Bohemian of the Year Award," The Pacific Repertory Theatre, Carmel, California

■ Co-Creator of *The Paterson-Colt Book: Featuring the Dennis A. LeVett Collection*

Printed in Great Britain
by Amazon